SAIR, SAIR WARK

Best wishes

Lillian King

WOMEN AND MINING IN SCOTLAND

LILLIAN KING

WINDFALL BOOKS

ISBN No: 0 9539839 0 0

Acknowledgements

For Belle, first last and always

I would like to express my gratitude to everyone who contributed
in any way to this book.

Special thanks go to
Ann Eden, Grace Mackinnon, Johan Cairns, Margaret Rodger, Barbara Marshall,
Margaret Wright and Jean Graham
Elsie Brodie and Linda Craig
Audrey Canning, STUC Library, Caledonian University, Glasgow
Sybil Cavanagh, Local History Headquarters, West Lothian
Elma Lindsay, Smith Museum & Art Gallery, Stirling
Neil Ballantyne, Summerlees Heritage Park, Coatbridge
Carol Sneddon, Callander House Museum, Falkirk
Ann Geddes, Baird Institute, Cumnock
Local History Staff at Dunfermline, Kirkcaldy, Falkirk and Alloa Libraries
James Robertson, for introducing me to the work of Hugh Miller
Guthrie Hutton for providing useful contacts
Helen Welsh for proof reading

Cover design by William Livingstone from a sketch in
the 1840 Children's Employment Commission

© Lillian King June 2001

The right of Lillian King to be identified as the author of this work has been asserted in
accordance with the Copyright, Designs and Patents Act 1988
A catalogue record for this book is available from the British Library

Printed by A4 Print Dunfermline
Typesetting, layout and design by Windfall Books
Published by Windfall Books, Kelty
01383 831076

SAIR, SAIR WARK
WOMEN AND MINING IN SCOTLAND

'It is sair , sair work, would like to be playing about better.'
Janet Allen, eight year old mine worker in Blairhall Colliery.

Countless books have been written about miners and mining, their appalling working conditions, their struggles with government and capitalists, their development from bonded slaves to law makers and legislators. Very little has been written from a woman's viewpoint but until the middle of the nineteenth century women shared the workplace with their husbands, brothers and fathers. In addition, throughout the whole history of mining, women have had to deal with the social, economic and health problems that were their share of an industry that powered the Industrial Revolution and brought untold wealth to the country.

Their contribution, as in so many areas of history, has been overlooked. This book is a small attempt to set the record straight. It is in no way a definitive work on the subject, but it may perhaps encourage other students to investigate this aspect of women's hidden history.

Lillian King June 2001

CONTENTS

INTRODUCTION

Before any discussion of women's role in coal mining can take place it is necessary to set the scene, to explore the background to what is a shameful and largely forgotten part of our history. That is hardly surprising because like most aspects of women's lives it has remained for centuries unwritten, with one notable exception. This came about by accident rather than intention. In 1840, seven years after the first Factory Acts limited the hours of work for children in factories, a commission was set up to investigate conditions of employment of children in mines, and for the first time the voices of women and girls were heard loud and clear. They described their lives and work in a factual, unemotional manner that shocked the entire nation; but the Commission did more than simply record their experiences, it provided sketches. The use of pictures was unique and drawings of women and children at work remain much more telling than mere words.

To be more accurate, this book should have as its title "Females and Scottish Mining" because for at least two hundred years, females between the ages of five and fifty worked as slaves underground to swell the coffers of government and line the pockets of landowners who owned the mineral rights beneath their green and pleasant land. Why fifty? Because, according to contemporary reports "they were generally extinct by that age" or if still alive, so severely crippled by injury or disease that any kind of work was impossible. [1]

Their land, consisting of mud and coal dirt, was by no means green and pleasant, their lives one long round of unceasing toil, their homes hovels without water or sanitation. So poor that the pennies earned by children were a necessary part of their income, these women, as well as the normal problems of child-bearing and caring, were forced to work underground for twelve to fifteen hours a day in conditions of unimaginable barbarity. They were the labourers, the carthorses of the pits, carrying on their backs loads of coal that took two men to lift or crawling, harnessed like oxen, to pull loaded waggons from the coal face to the pit bottom. They had to cope with disease and injury to themselves and their families, and death and disaster were always close neighbours.

In this century, such is the desire for equality that the 1989 Employment Act made it possible for women to work underground again and in America, women have gone to court to defend their right to work as miners. They, at least, have the luxury of choice as well as reasonably clean and safe working conditions. The women whose lives were ruled both by sheer economic necessity and the demands of the coal masters were not so lucky. For them, equality consisted of the right to work or starve alongside their men.

The 1840 Commission uncovered evidence which was received on one hand with incredulity and on the other with a desperate attempt to deny its accuracy. Mine owners made light of hardships, claiming that if miners wanted to live in squalor and take children down the pit as soon as they were old enough to walk, there was no reason for them to interfere. Even the commissioners who expressed horror at working conditions, condemned the lack of furniture and cleanliness in the coal company houses. They did not seem to realise that what people earned was scarcely enough to keep them alive, let alone provide luxuries like proper beds and solid furniture. In Victorian Britain, the lack of cleanliness was seen to be almost as big a sin as ungodliness, but when pits were in production twenty four hours a day and members of families worked on different shifts, it was impossible to keep the home free from wet and dirty working clothes. Nevertheless women working a fourteen hour day in backbreaking toil were condemned for not upholding family values.

Much of the commission's report, quoted verbatim from the evidence given by women and children, so shocked and horrified the nation that immediate steps were taken to banish the practice of employing females underground. This would free them from servitude both from the coal owners and from the husbands and fathers who used a strap to control girls who did not come up to the required workhorse standards.

Until laws were passed to enable miners to become free men in 1779, babies were sold into slavery at baptism for a few pennies or some goods in kind and over sixty years later, miners families remained slaves in fact if not in law. Fife and the Lothians were, together, one of the worst areas in the country, with appalling records of death and injury and the simplicity of speech of young, uneducated girls being interviewed is in shocking contrast to what they are describing.

Many people in mining villages today will be direct descendants of these women and must know that, even in this century, their villages were seen as mere backwaters of civilisation, to be avoided at all costs; that miners and their families were strange subhuman people who had little contact with, or little in common with people in other employment. What they probably don't know is that this difference was imposed on them by the government and the reason they don't know it is because it was kept hidden. Writing in 1909, Tom Johnson said that this was the fault of the historian:

> *'What he knew of happenings calculated to cast odium on our landed gentry, he carefully excised from the records and, where he did not know, he was careful to assume and to lead others to assume that the periods of which he was ignorant were periods of intense social happiness wherein a glad and thankful populace spent their days and nights devising Hallelujahs in honour of the neighbouring nobleman - and that is why the history of Scottish mining is wrapped in darkness ; that is why we never hear of two hundred years of slavery ; why the collier of today does not know that his ancestor of a century ago was a two-legged chattel, bought, sold and lashed as were the cotton plantation slaves in pre- civil war times in the USA.* '[2]

Miners, and that term includes men, women and children of all ages, were denied access to education, an act of 1616 specifically excluding them. They were also excluded from the Habeas Corpus Act, which meant that, unlike anyone else in the country, they could be imprisoned indefinitely without trial. In life, miners were treated as less than human, bonded slaves for centuries after serfdom had been abolished in the rest of the country, sacrificed to the gods of national economy and personal wealth. Even after death, the miner remained outside society. In some parts of the country, tradition has it that he could not be buried in the same ground as free men but had his grave in unconsecrated ground. Today this knowledge is more wide spread though the extent to which women and children were enslaved is not so well understood, but the sense of oneness, of common cause that brought women on to the picket lines in the last great battles against the Thatcher regime was forged over these bad years. Even now, when the industry has been destroyed, the sense of close community and sisterhood is apparent to a degree not found elsewhere. Nowadays, if you mention women and mines, it is the picture of picket lines that is evoked, or that of the soup kitchen. Newspaper pictures of these abound and women have been seen only as peripheral, their role that of nurturing and supporting their men folk, but if Churchill had succeeded in sending in the tanks, as he threatened to do in times of strike, the women would have been among the first to stand up in front of them.

Soup kitchen workers. Elizabeth Forster from Denbeath on right.

Bannockburn Soup Kitchen 1926

Peeling potatoes for mass meals Methil soup kitchen 1926

CHAPTER ONE

SLAVERY

Mining has a long history. Next to hunting and food gathering it is probably one of man's oldest skills, and as long as ten thousand years ago flint was mined for making tools. Miners had their own patron saint, Barbara, who also looked after firemen and quarrymen, and coal is mentioned in the Bible. In Leviticus, Chapter 16 verse 12, Aaron is instructed to present a bull as a sin offering for himself and to make atonement for his house -'and he shall take a censer full of coals of fire from off the altar and two handfuls of sweet incense.' Coal may have been mined on the Forth and Clyde rivers in Roman times. Records remain from the 12th century of coal workings by the monks of Newbattle and Holyrood Abbeys. At the same time, coal was in such regular use that Berwick had regulations governing its sale and in 1292, the monks of Dunfermline were given rights to dig coal for their own use but not for sale. After a visit to Newbattle in 1435, Pope Aeneas Silvius wrote that poor people were given black stone as alms by the monks there instead of money. Monks were Scotland's first coal miners but they could never have envisaged the misery their work would lead to.

From earliest times, miners were treated differently from other members of society. In 1364,[1] an act to abolish slavery was passed by the Scottish Parliament but miners and their families were excluded because they were regarded as necessary servants, obliged to work and to be bought and sold along with the colliery. Sixty years later, when mining was seen to be a lucrative undertaking, all mines became the property of the king who retained the right to a tenth of all profits when ownership was eventually returned to the landowners.

For a hundred years and more after Queen Elizabeth freed all English miners from serfdom, a series of acts were passed tightening the bonds of slavery in Scotland. Miners children were bound for life to the colliery while masters were given the right to suspend workers, seize their belongings, and to punish and imprison them for perceived wrongdoing. In 1592 an act of Parliament declared that setting fire to a coal bank was treason, and John Henry was found guilty of 'the crime of setting fire to the coal heugh of Fawside'. Hanged at the Market Cross in Edinburgh, his head was sent to Fawside where it was placed on a pole beside the mine as a warning. [2]

By 1661, every person employed by a coal owner, either on the surface or below ground was in bondage, to be accounted for among the rest of his master's property, waggons, tools, horses etc. and was held to be of less value then any of these and more expendable. In 1770, an advertisement in the Caledonian Mercury offered for sale in Edinburgh 'seams of coal within Halbeath.... with the whole of the machinery, colliery houses, colliers and pertinents thereof...'

Records from the Rothes Estates show that miners had to sign a document which asked, 'Are you satisfied to serve the Earl of Rothes and his family as their bound coallier and that not only yourself but yours?' [3] He had to agree to work wherever his master thought fit to put him, and to buy all his meal from his lordship at above market price. In addition, the miner had to supply his master with one free load of coal each week, which meant in effect that for part of every week, he worked for nothing. Mine owners could dictate the collier's private as well as working life. A contract dated 1777 outlined the conditions of employment of a miner, George Pickard. He had to undertake not to commit fornication, get married, waste his master's goods, play cards or dice or haunt taverns and playhouses.[4] Lord Cockburn, writing shortly after the miners were freed, said that 'while collier or salter slaves could not legally be killed or directly tortured by their masters, in every other respect they were held to be as cattle, possessing no human rights.' [5] As late as 1820, Robert Bald could write about the owner of the Clyde Iron Works who had in his possession a slave he had acquired in exchange for a donkey. [6]

How long women have actually worked in mining is impossible to guess, but the earliest known record refers to a woman losing her life at a lead mine in Derbyshire after a firedamp explosion in 1322.[7] In 1587, because of a shortage of local labour during a dispute between a mine owner in Newcastle and the Earl of Westmoreland, Scottish men and women miners were employed at Winlaton Colliery.[8] Twenty years later, hundreds of women and children were labouring underground.

How could such a situation come about? The answer was, as it usually is, money and greed. In earlier times, mines had been worked where outcrops were close to the surface but the practice of deep mining by ladders and shafts meant that, by 1590, during the reign of James VI, a lot of money had been invested in bigger and deeper pits.

[Harnessed Putters in Mid Lothian.]

The export trade was so flourishing that complaints were made of a shortage of coal at home. In 1595, John Napier, the inventor of logarithms, whose name is commemorated in Napier University in Edinburgh, devised a scheme for pumping water out of mine workings, so providing a solution for one of the greatest problems of deep pit mining. The other, the need for an enormous labour force was solved by the simple expedient of forcing people into work in the mines. This was possible because a vast pool of people existed whose lives had been disrupted by the Reformation and the dissolution of the monasteries.

In 1559, John Knox had preached a sermon in Perth about idolatry, inciting a mob to attack and destroy religious houses in the city and the spirit of destruction spread all over the country. The church was certainly corrupt but controlled much of the wealth of the country and provided a kind of security for the settlements which grew up alongside the monasteries. With their dissolution, the social life of the country was disrupted and many people, through no fault of their own, were destitute, forced to become vagrants and beggars or dependent on the Poor Law for their survival. The Poor Law of 1579 recognised the existence of the poor and infirm and tried to deal with the problem but had neither the will nor the ability to cope with the huge mass of 'able-bodied poor'. It ordained that people with no means of support were to be convicted, branded or whipped, but the sentence could be commuted to service with an employer for a year. All coal heugh and salt pan owners were instructed to 'apprehend and put to labour all sturdy beggars'. The Act was amended in 1597 so that beggars' children could be seized and kept in bondage, that is, they were slaves, tied to their masters, till the age of eighteen for females and twenty four for males.

One reason for the introduction of this bonding system was to prevent coal owners from 'poaching' workers from other mines. According to Lord Cockburn, 'this ensured that wives, daughters and sons went on from generation to generation under the system which was the family doom.' [9]

From an Act in 1641 we learn that colliers had been in the habit of taking holidays at 'Pasche, Yoole and Witsonday' a practice which the Act condemned as 'to the great offence of God and the prejudice of their maisters'. So holidays such as Easter and Whitsun were abolished and miners had to work six days a week, because it was believed that any time off was spent in drink and debauchery and that men were unable to work efficiently the next day. The Yuletide holiday was retained because December 25th was a quarter day and traditionally that was when all 'flitting and entering' took place but six years later, the law was changed so that all flitting had to take place on December the first and anyone celebrating Yule or 'any other superstitious days' could be punished. This was in line with laws against 'the profanation of the Sabbath.' [10] A common punishment for wrongdoing was the jougs, iron collars which fastened round the wrongdoer's neck and were attached to a wall, and the man could be 'nailed to a prop at the pit bottom for a whole day at least'. The common practice was for the laird or tackman to choose the place of work and 'if we did not do his bidding we were placed by the neck in iron collars called juggs or made to go the rown. The latter I recollect well - the men's hands were tied facing the horse at the gin and made to run round backward all day. Sometimes the horse was released and the man had to push the gin, winding the wagons of coal up to the pit head'. [11]

The people who enforced the laws were the landowners with all the wealth of the coal beneath their feet so they were quick to take advantage and, as local magistrates, they were able to ensure that punitive measures were brought in. Once employed as a coal miner or coal bearer, a man could not look for another job without permission from his master. If he did, the master had the power to seek him out and bring him back. Anyone employing a runaway miner was forced to give him up or pay one hundred pounds Scots for every time of asking and a deserting miner was looked on as a thief because he had stolen himself away from his owner so would be punished for his crime. Con-victed criminals also provided a pool of unwilling employees. In 1701, Alexander Stewart was sentenced to death for theft but had his sentence commuted and he was gifted to Sir John Erskine of Alloa as a 'perpetual and un-restricted slave'. [12] This sentence was inscribed on a metal collar which was riveted round his neck.

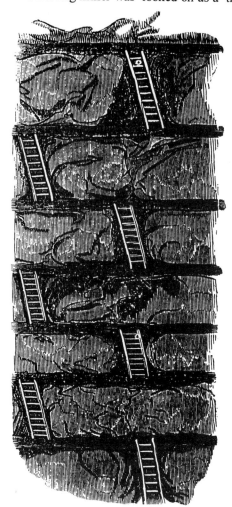

Though miners weren't free to move, it was acceptable and in-deed common practice, for own-ers to more them around if need be. In 1713, the Earl of Rothes 'borrowed' some colliers from Dunfermline to work his mines. Lord Wemyss lent a number of colliers to Balfour of Balbirnie and later wrote asking for their return 'as I have present occa-sion for them and as soon as I can spare any again, you shall have them.' [13]

18th century ladder pit

When a miner, Walter Cowan and Elizabeth Japp, presumably his wife, 'absconded' from Fordell, he was charged with 'endeavouring to raise mutinies or other distur- bances' and imprisoned in The Tolbooth in Edinburgh. Two miners had to stand as guarantors of his return to his master's work and also for Elizabeth 'who likewise be- longed to Fordell works'. [14] Workers did not always bow to the inevitable but any attempt at protest was put down ruthlessly , with all the strength of the law and the help of the military if need be. In 1742 the following warrant [15] was issued by the factor of the Rothes Estate:

PETITION AND WARRANT

FROM THE SHERIFF

to the persons of

JAMES CAIRNS and JAMES FORTUNE, COLLIERS

To The Sheriff of Fife and his Deputy.

The Petition of William Hay, Factor to the Earle of Rothes.

Herewith

That James Fortune and James Cairnes two Coallyers belonging to the said Earle and properly employed in working the Coall of Cadham have turned so obstroperous that they refused to work at the said Coall at the ordinary rate the rest of the Coallyers at said work got and even tho' their wadges have been considerably advanced .They threaten to leave the work which will not only be a great loss to the proprietor of the Coall but of verry bad example to the rest of his Coallyers and even to others in the neighbourhood.

May it please your Lordship to grant Warrant for Committing the said James Fortune and James Cairnes prisoners within the Tolbooth of Cupar therein to remain till they find sufficient caution to perform and abide at their work as formerly and as the other neighbouring Coallyers are made to do according to justice.

A mutiny in 1752 by miners on the Earl Of Rothes estates led to three miners being imprisoned in Kirkcaldy and several others in the Tolbooth in Cupar as the following account shows:

ACCOUNT OF EXPENSES OF IMPRISONING CLUNIE COLLIERS	£	s	d
Drink money to a party of soldiers who apprehended them		1	
To the officers Servt.		1	
Stabling Mr. Rolland's Horse			3
To each of three Soldiers That Carried the Coaliers to Coupar prison 2/-		6	
To a Corporal		3	
To each of 5 soldiers that Carried 3 Coaliers to Kirkcaldy 1/6		7	6
To a Corporal		2	
To each of 2 Sherriffmairs as fees and to bear their charges from Clunie, the one to Coupar, the other to Kirkcaldie 2/6		5	
Paid the gaoler at Cupar for maintainance of Coaliers Sent to Cupar		11	1
Consigned at Kirkcaldie for the prisoners maintenance		10	6
	2	7	4

Another memorandum dealing with two absconding miners demands:

'That the two Hasties be enquired after and apprehended as soon as they can be got. That the Coalliers or their Wives who shall be mutinous or Abusive to their Neighbours in interrupting them at their work shall be imprisoned untill they acknowledge their fault. That Somebody be sent down twice or thrice a week to Enquire if Everybody be at work and behaving well.' [16]

Slavery is an old story, and has always been endemic throughout the world. Under Roman law, children born to slaves were born into servitude, and so too were the later American plantation slaves. In Scotland, slavery was not hereditary, children were born free but were bonded by their fathers. This was brought about by a species of bribery. A man would bind himself and his children to a coal owner by taking 'arles', that is, earnest money or goods. In other words by accepting this 'gift', he was in effect pledging himself and his family to the service of mine owner. The value of the 'gift' is shown in this example from 1748 when, at Prestongrange in East Lothian, 'There were entered and bound to the coal works, William and Helen Taits, by giving each of them a pair of new shoes on earnest at one shilling and nine pence a pair.' [17] The custom grew of arling children to the coal master, not when they were old enough to work but when they were baptised. It was a formal contract, witnessed by the minister and meant that the child had, in effect, been sold to the mine owner. Later on, it was accepted that the child was bound for life even if not arled, by the mere fact of assisting its father in his work. This system was not destroyed till 1799, when the miners were freed, officially at least, from slavery.

Slave labour came to an end because of the industrial revolution. The rapid development of factories and iron works created an enormous demand for coal and the existing work force was neither large enough, nor efficient enough to cater for that demand. New workers were needed, but jobs in other industries were available and no-one would submit to slavery when there were other alternatives. Before agreeing to become colliers, this new work force demanded - and was granted - not only freedom of choice but higher wages than they could get any where else.

By then, a change of attitude was apparent, though this came about only when it appeared to be expedient. In 1774, the Earl of Abercorn and other mine owners brought about a bill to free the miners, the preamble of which spelled out the position of mining families in society - 'whereas by the statute law of Scotland, as explained by the judges of the courts of law there, many colliers and coal bearers and salters are in a state of slavery or bondage, bound to the collieries or salt works where they work, transferable with the collieries and salt works. [18] The Bill was passed the following year despite the objections of many owners who petitioned against it. The coal owners reasons for objecting were economic, knowing that they owned vast, untapped sources of wealth which they believed would remain so without a large and docile work force. The motives of those proposing the bill were identical to those of the objectors but they were quicker to see the benefits of a fluid population where market forces would be supreme, and gave their machinations a gloss of philanthropy. The bill stated that it would end the disgrace of 'a state of servitude in a free country.' In other words, they were happy to go along with the system while it was working in their favour, and equally happy to drop it when it was not. Thomas Johnston wrote that, 'the miner slave was freed in the same holy cause in which he was enslaved - the cause of low wages.' [19]

So, the miners were free. Or were they? It certainly wasn't instant emancipation. New workers coming into the industry would remain free, of course, but those already employed were still bound to their masters. Those under twenty were to be set free after seven years, as were those between thirty five and forty five – on condition that they trained an apprentice in the 'art or mystery of coal hewing.' If they didn't, another three years were added to their sentence. Over forty fives were freed in three years, but in all cases, if a miner took part in a strike for higher wages or left his place of employment before his liberation day, he had to serve another two years as punishment. For the rest, freedom could take between five and ten years. Women and children were to be liberated at the same time as the head of the family, but in practice, this was no simple matter.

Freedom from serfdom was not automatic, the miner having to sue his master in the Sheriff Court, a proceeding beyond the power of men who could neither read nor write, and those who gained their freedom entered into another form of slavery, that of debt. The arles, paid to the father at the christening of his children were, because the mine owner was deprived of their labour, treated as a debt which had to be discharged before a miner could be free. With a large family, and having received loans to cover times of sickness and hardship, most miners owed a debt they could never repay. Better paid jobs were out of the question because a new master would have to pay off the debt to the old one before taking on his employee.

When a bill to amend the 1795 act was introduced, there was a tacit acceptance that the earlier bill had not achieved what it set out to do. It declared that 'notwithstanding the former act, many colliers and bearers still continue in a state of bondage'. Colliery owners organised petitions against it, and in 1799 when all colliers became free and equal before the law and wages were fixed by Justices of the Peace, many miners celebrated by becoming labourers at half the wages they had in the pits. Freedom is relative, however, and equality in law did not equate with freedom from economic necessity, and slavery, though no longer the official policy of the British government continued to survive.......

Until horse gins were introduced women worked the windlass
bringing workers and coal to the surface

CHAPTER TWO

WIVES AND DAUGHTERS

It is said that though men make their own history, they do not make it as they please
or under circumstances of their own choosing. If this is true for men, how much more
so it is for women; the circumstances in which women in mining communities lived
and worked provide a horrifying picture of their role on the borders of humanity.
Mine and factory proprietors owned other people's children and were quite happy to
employ little girls for up to fourteen hours a day as human cart horses while their own
offspring of the same age were still being treated as babies. But the mine owners
could not have succeeded in the domination of women and children without the tacit
consent of the miners themselves. Wives and daughters, as well as being bound to the
mine owner, were the unpaid slaves of fathers and husbands, coal bearers who
worked underground, carrying loads from the coal face to the bottom of the shaft or
climbing up ladders to the surface. They also carried the burden of providing for the
family when the man was unable or unwilling to work. The only women receiving
money were 'fremit' bearers, those working for a contractor, a man who was not related to them. They belonged to the coal master but he could give them, sometimes on
a year's lease, to a miner who would 'bind himself' to give the bearer proper work
and wages during the term of her engagement.' [1] These women had no rights but
had to go wherever in the mine they were sent,and cope with beatings, bad temper
and whatever load they were given to carry without complaint. They did tell the
commissioners, however, that they were 'sore driven.'
A man without wife or children had to pay a woman to carry for him, but those with
families had a band of unpaid helpers. Until the nineteenth century females were usually employed only on coal carrying, although in some places girls worked at the coal
seams with a pick like other miners and an account remains of a Lochgelly woman
who was more than a match for her male fellow workers. (see p20). By the 1840s ,
however, it is likely that the use of women and children underground was on the
wane as many areas where it had been the practice no longer employed females. Before the nineteenth century there were women working underground in Ayrshire and
Lanarkshire but by 1840 only Fife, Lothian and Clackmannan employed a considerable number.
Much of our knowledge of conditions in the coal mines comes from the 1840 Children's Employment Commission. As governments became aware of intolerable working conditions in factories in the new industrial towns, a series of Acts was passed to
restrict hours of work, though these provisions were largely ignored, and did not apply at all in the mining industry. However, an inspector sent to inquire into the workings of the Factory Acts decided to extend his inquiry into the state of the colliery
population in his area. The resulting publicity, which outlined the physical and mental condition of the few miners children attending school, attracted the attention of

Lord Shaftesbury, who then set up a commission of inquiry.

No-one could have foreseen the furore this caused or even imagined the enormity of evils it disclosed. Tiny children too frail to walk, were carried on the backs of parents to conserve their little strength for working underground. Though collieries were small many people died in explosions and children as young as five appeared prominently in accounts of death and injury though there were no official statistics. Inquiries into accident and sudden death were unheard of, even in cases where murder was suspected. No official records were kept; there were no laws to protect children and many fathers insisted that families would starve without the contribution of even the smallest children. Evidence existed, though, of men working only three or four days a week instead of six. As long as members of a miner's family were doing his job, the mine owner had no complaint against him.

Evidence for the Commission was taken from child labourers, parents, adult workers, teachers, doctors and ministers. Employers, too, were interviewed but much of their evidence was found to be suspect, claiming working days of six to seven hours instead of the customary eleven to twelve hours. Owners were also unwilling to admit to employing seven year olds, insisting that the normal starting age was between eight and nine. They also claimed to have no control over the number of children down the pit at any one time and in fact, children of four and five years were found working and from six years of age the work of dragging or pushing loaded carts from the coal face to the shaft began. Mine owners accepted no necessity for interfering or responsibility for children who were under the care of their natural guardians. If their fathers didn't mind them working, why should the owners?

It is necessary to put things into perspective. Children had always worked, as a matter of course, even toddlers being pressed into service as soon as they were able to lend a

Putting in East and Midlothian

hand. In agricultural areas children of four or five were employed as bird scarers, to herd sheep and cows and prevent them from straying onto ploughed fields. It is likely that the pattern of whole family employment continued when the agricultural background gave way to the industrial, but what could be seen as acceptable in a domestic situation, where children were under the direct control of the mother, ceased to be so when the emphasis of work moved out from the home.

In towns, children worked in factories rather than in home-based industries and work-houses regularly sold orphan children to the new cotton mills. Children as young as five were used to clean machinery because they were small enough to crawl under the machines to remove the waste and dust. It was the development of huge concentrations of factories, however, using pauper children as slaves, many of them sold as job lots at auction, that increased child labour and child mortality to the point where government action became necessary to regulate it. A child of two was found working in a lace manufacturers and three year olds carried bricks at a brickworks. Conditions in factories and sweat shops were dreadful, but even the worst factory could not begin to compare with conditions underground.

Among the conclusions of the Commission was that among mine workers, crippled and distorted bodies were common, that seeds of painful and mortal illness were sown in childhood and that each generation of 'this class of population was commonly extinct soon after fifty.' John Weir, a forty eight year old coal hewer at Elgin Colliery said he had been off work for eight years with the black spit, that ten out of every twenty men had it by the age of twenty and were dead before forty. He was unable to get money from the poor rates because his 'little ones' worked down below. 'Without them, he says, 'the younger ones and I would starve'. The Means Test was so strict that if even one child in the family was working, no payment would be made. In one parish, where thirty five families, one hundred and eighty five persons altogether were destitute, the amount paid out in poor relief was five shillings.

There were some in the industry who claimed to be concerned about conditions of employment. The ninth Earl of Dundonald banned women from his pits before 1790, denouncing the 'barbarous and ultimately expensive method of converting colliers wives and daughters into beasts of burden.' [2] At the same time, he complained about the 'extravagant wages' earned by colliers. In 1808, Robert Bald had published his 'Inquiry into condition of those women who carry coals underground in Scotland by the name of bearers.' His findings persuaded the Earl of Mar to ban women workers at his Alloa Coal Company, but miners objected so fiercely that the ban was restricted to married women only. The Duke of Buccleugh also banned women from his pits before 1842 but with no law to back it up his ban was largely ignored. Some collieries employed only single women and at Plean Muir in Stirling only children over twelve were allowed underground.

The mine manager of the Elgin Colliery believed that very young children were not necessary but 'are cheaper and soon become a benefit to their parents.' This pit did not allow married women to work but employed sixty female adults, thirty six of those under eighteen and nine children, the youngest being nine years old. Henry Chisholm, manager of the Lochgelly Pit said that 'our seams of coal, being thick, five to eight feet, very young children are not needed.' He employed ten children under the age of thirteen but their time was limited to twelve hours and no night work was allowed. No married women worked in his mine and some Fife pits, like Dysart and Thornton, refused to employ women at all.

The owner of Drumcarra Colliery at Cameron claimed that 'No females have ever wrought in this part of Fife', but these pits were the tiny exception to the general rule. There were a few owners far-sighted enough to see the benefit of banning women from mine workings - better quality of child care, better health and life style. The owner of Clunie Colliery claimed that no females whatever worked in his pits. 'Keeping them out,' he said, 'is one of the most important points towards the im-provement of the collier population, as it forces them to self-dependence. Their daughters are sent to the fields or into service and marry millers, ploughmen etc. so miners have to seek wives from other trades.'

Unfortunately such men represented a minority of owners. More common was the be-lief expressed by a teacher who said that 'no particular advantage would be gained by excluding women from the pit as they are used to the work and fit for nothing else and it might increase the cost of coal by two pence or two pence halfpenny a ton.'

Many owners claimed that ending female labour would deprive them of their best

Putting in Fife and Clackmannanshire

workers and that girls, as a rule, began work younger than boys because they learned to be useful earlier. One of the worst pits appears to be Fordell Colliery, or perhaps the manager there was more honest in reporting that girls began to help 'draw by the chain from six years old and many from six to twelve are employed in pumping and carrying water from six in the morning till six in the evening.'

These 'pumpers' were boys and girls whose business was to 'descend into the deepest part of the mine to pump rising water to the level of the engine pump in order to keep the men's rooms of work dry.' The children worked in cramped conditions, up to their waists and sometimes almost covered with water, working six hours on and twelve off, which meant continually varying shifts. These were not the youngest children; apart from carrying coal as part of the family group, four to five year olds were, because of their size, employed as trappers. They spent hours alone, in the dark, opening and shutting air doors to ventilate the pit.

There were several categories of female worker. Putters dragged or pushed loaded carts weighing from three to ten hundred weights from the coal face to the pit bottom, while strappers were girls who were yoked like oxen and 'harnessed over the shoulders and back with a strong leather girth' with an iron hook which was attached to a chain fastened to the coal cart. The girls wore dresses made of canvas that was very quickly saturated where the ground was wet, some had heavy iron shod shoes but most were barefoot. A variation of the harness meant that straps went round the girls waist and she pulled the cart backwards, but whichever method was used, all had to struggle over rough ground or roadways inches deep in mud and up steep slopes.

Drawing the slype was harder than pulling wheeled waggons.
The narrow seams meant that girls had to crawl

Sometimes the carts were equipped with basic iron runners, others had wheels, but in places where seams were narrow, everyone had to crawl backwards and forwards in spaces sometimes less than thirty inches high. Without the sketches made at the time, it would be impossible to imagine these scenes underground.

The job of the coal-bearer was to carry loads of coal up to three hundred weights on her back up and down steep braes, and in the case of ladder pits, up a series of ladders to the surface. William Fyfe, the overseer at Castle Bigg Colliery described the work of the five women employed there: 'Two women drive the coal on hurlies below ground and three carry the coals on their backs to the surface. The roads are the same height as the coal face i.e. about three to four feet, they then ascend the stair-pit to the day which is thirteen fathoms high'.

In some deeper pits, it is reckoned that women and girls climbed heights equivalent to that of a modern multi-storey block of flats, not once but many times a day. As well as being hard work, this could be extremely dangerous. Agnes Moffat, who started work underground at the age of ten said that sometimes while climbing ladders the straps which went round the forehead to secure the load would break and the load fall on the girl following, causing death or serious injury. Accidents in all parts of the pit were commonplace but were seen as unimportant. Thomas Bishop, the overseer at Polkemmet Colliery said that 'few accidents had occurred lately. We have no record of accidents, nor is it customary to keep such, not even accidental and sudden deaths.' Mr Marshall from Netherwood Colliery said it was not the custom to notice these accidents. 'We neither give notice nor do the friends of the parties. The practice is to bury them a day or so after their decease.'

Occasionally the sheriff took an interest. After the death of a man caused by an overwind, he inspected the ropes, examined their strength and walked away. No further notice was taken. From the nature of the work, minor accidents were inevitable but commissioners were not prepared for the amount of general apathy and indifference. Ann Ranger broke both ankles, Jane Fyfe had an arm crushed by a wagon and twelve year old Mary McLean was off work for a year after both legs were crushed. Girls were caught by runaway wagons, fell down the shaft and many deaths were caused by roof and coal falls and by explosions.

[Load dropping on ladder while ascending.]

Owners paid little attention to death and disaster as long as the mine continued to function and revenue wasn't lost. Any complaint was answered by the assertion that the master made his own laws and men must go by them, not by what his neighbours might be doing. The Earl of Wemyss, the coal owning MP for Fife said he 'had a perfect right to keep his coal pits filled with black damp if he so chose.' He forced nobody to go into his pits and nobody was at liberty to constrain him to act otherwise than as he thought proper. [3]

CHAPTER THREE

SAIR SWEATIN WARK

Back breaking labour was not restricted to women in mining areas. In agricultural communities they were also treated like pack horses, carrying everything from grain, hay and manure in creels on their backs.Legend has it that gangs of women were employed to raise the earthen ramparts of Edward the First's castles in Scotland. Women worked in lead and silver mines but if they worked underground in other mining areas in Britain apart from Fife, the Lothians, Clackmannan and Stirlingshire, the practice had died out by the beginning of the eighteenth century.

In 1724 a mining engineer from Newcastle was surprised to learn from Sir John Clerk of Penicuik that he employed women as bearers. Geological problems were given as the reason - 'the coals of Loanhead lye all dipping exceedingly so that it is not easy to command them by an engine.' [1] One hundred years later, Matthias Dunn wrote that 'It is difficult to account for a system so replete with poverty, shame and demoralisation and , moreover, so destitute of real economy.' [2] How many women and children were actually employed below ground is impossible to estimate with any degree of accuracy. Census returns are notoriously faulty, which is hardly surprising with a largely illiterate population. Mine owners employed one man but he was 'assisted' by a wife and several children who did not necessarily appear on official records.

Women's work was seen as normal and acceptable and girls married young. In her evidence to the 1840 Commission, Janet Selkirk said that 'Men only marry us early because we are an advantage to them.' An old collier, born in 1768, said he'd been 'obliged to marry early to avoid paying out all the money he earned as a hewer.' Over a hundred years later, when women were no longer employed as bearers, girls were held at a discount in mining areas. Girl babies were referred to as 'a hutch of dross' and boy babies as 'a hutch of coals' [3] but in 1842, girls were more valuable than boys because they started work earlier and were more biddable. Girls, however, were fit only for the unskilled but arduous work of bearing coal. Boys were trained in coal hewing by their fathers who jealously guarded mining as a closed industry and its 'mystery' was handed down through the generations.

The Commission had no remit to investigate women's work experience so the investigators must have been horrified enough by what they found, to include their evidence. They talked to a fifty year old female coal hewer and a widow who claimed she had carried coal till the age of sixty six. With tied houses, widows usually had to work until their children were old enough to take over as the main breadwinner.

Archibald Cook, who was born in 1837, listed Hannah Hodge among the eight miners employed at Lochgelly. Between them they produced ten tons of coal daily. The women regularly carried about a hundredweight of coal on their shoulders and Hannah Hodge and another miner, Janet Erskine had a trial of strength when they each carried four hundredweight. Their weekly wage was six shillings and they saw day-light only on a Sunday. These women had to be tough.

'If anything went wrong with the man such as sickness or death, the woman had to be both miner and bearer,' wrote Cook, " such was the case with my grandmother. She was left a widow with five young children and no way of supporting them , only by her own hand. My father was only four months old and my uncle two years. Her three girls were older. There was nothing for her to do but to go and dig her coals. She carried the infant children down the pit, laid them at the stoop side until she dug her coals and carried it to the pit bank. When she rested she gave my father a drink and my uncle a spoonful of cold mashed potatoes. Oatmeal and potatoes provided all their living in those days. The only light she had was the reflection from fish heads. As they grew up her family carried the coals and redd. My father started at eight years of age .'

Sir Gilbert Elliot, the owner of the mine is quoted as saying that she 'brought more coal to the bank than any miner at his works'. [4]

When a windlass replaced the women carrying the coal to the pit head, production increased to fifteen tons a day, but there was no ease for the women. They had to work the windlass until horse gins were introduced.

Workers being drawn up the shaft by horse gin

The best description of work in the mines come from the women and children themselves. The recurring theme is that girls are forced to go down the pit by their fathers, that they hate the work but can't run away from it. Some like Janet Neilson, who was in service, were persuaded that they would earn more and therefore be of more use to the family if they worked underground. Few had any choice in the matter, as Janet Cumming, eleven year old coal bearer explained:

' I gang with the women at five and come up at five at night; work all night on Fridays and come away at twelve in the day. The roof is very low; I have to bend my back and legs and the water is frequently up to the calves of my legs. Have no liking for the work. Father makes me like it.'

Isabella Read, twelve years old could not say how many rakes (journeys) she made from pit bottom to wall-face and back but thought about twenty five to thirty; the distance varying from a hundred to two hundred and fifty fathoms. 'When first down, I fell asleep while waiting for coal from heat and fatigue. I do not like the work, nor do the lassies but are made to like it. When the weather is warm, there is difficulty breathing and frequently the lights go out.'

Fourteen year old Elizabeth Brown drew carts of coal to the horse road and worked between eleven and twelve hours a day. At Wellwood Colliery sixty six children were drawing coal below ground. They normally began work at ten years old, but could be taken earlier 'if destitute'. Twelve year old Elizabeth Gibb drew corves with chains but was not harnessed, holding the chain in both hands and drawing forward like a horse. Grace Cook had been doing the job for nine years since she was seven. At Hill of Beath, colliers 'worked their children at eight and nine years'. Sixteen year old Catherine Walker was unusual in that she didn't start work till she was ten but often worked eighteen hours on a double shift. Her father was dead and there were five children in the family.

Agnes Moffat, seventeen years old said that she 'began working at ten years of age, work twelve to fourteen hours daily, can earn twelve shillings in a fortnight, if work be not stopped by bad air. Father took sister and I down, he gets our wages.'

Katharine Logan, sixteen years old, had been carrying coal for more than five years and now worked in harness, 'drawing backward with face to tubs. The ropes and chains go under pit clothes, it is o'er sair work, especially when we crawl.'

Katharine Logan

Many children had bald patches on their heads where they pushed heavy wagons and injury and disablement were accepted as a normal part of their working lives. Girls fell from ladders when ropes holding baskets broke and coal fell on them from above, while others were hurt by runaway waggons or fell down pit shafts.

Helen Read, sixteen years old, had been for five years in one pit, working ' from five in the morning till six at night and carry two hundredweight on my back. I dinna like the work but think I'm fit for none other. Many accidents happen below ground. I've met with two serious ones myself. Two years ago the pit closed on thirteen of us and we were two days without food and light. Nearly one day we were up to our chins in water. At last we picked our way to an old shaft and were heard by people working above.'

Mary McLean, twelve years old, began work at eight, worked three years below but was off for twelve months with crushed legs. The injury was caused by the drag breaking as the cart holding six hundredweights was coming down a steep brae.

'It is sair, sair work, would like to be playing about better,' said Janet Allen. Eight years old, she had been working in Blair Colliery with her two sisters for nine months helping to push tubs.

Hard as it is to believe, some girls actually chose to work in the colliery. Helen Weir, sixteen years old, started working in a factory at nine but left after three years because she couldn't cope with the dust and her legs swelled with having to stand for long periods. She needed to work only eight to nine hours in the pit and could earn fourteen pence a day, though two pence of that went on oil and cotton for her lamp. Isabella Burt also claimed that though the work was sore, the hours were shorter than other places and that left time for tambour work which gave them a little extra income. Other girls made stockings on days there was no work but Helen Spowart said that coal bearing was ' very heavy cloughty work and am never able to do muckle after hours because of fatigue.'

An orphan, she lived with her brothers and stepmother, who was too old to work. Helen would have preferred to find other work 'but canna gang as stepmother would be put out of the house.'

According to Mary Morgan the work consisted of having to make fifty to sixty rakes daily. The roads were six hundred to nine hundred metres long, had low roofs so girls were forced to stoop all the time, 'and the brae is awful steep, the sweat drops off like streams of water'. Isabel Hugh, nineteen years old, was unusual in that she worked on her own account with a female partner so actually earned some money for the twelve to fourteen hour daily grind of 'guid sair, sweating work.'

It was easier for girls if they were on a daily rate, but if being paid by results, 'the men drive us more.' It is important to remember that it was not the mine owner who did the driving, that in mines where women were banned, working conditions improved considerably, roads were better, the height of passageways raised and coal production increased, but this knowledge was not widespread .

Twelve year old Mary McKinley worked for a contractor for a shilling a day, eleven days a fortnight with only a half hour break 'at porridge time.' Jane Kerr, twelve years old, said she got up at three in the morning and went to work at four, returning at four or five at night. 'I never get porridge before my return home but I bring a bit of oatcake and get water when thirsty. The ladder pit I work in is gai drippie and the air is kind of bad as the lamps do na burn sa bright as in guid air.'

Where the air was bad, fish heads were used to give a glimmer of light and added to the putrid atmosphere. Margaret Watson, sixteen years old, was first taken below to carry coals when she was six years old. ' We often have bad air, had some a short time since and lost brother by it. He sunk down and I tried to draw him out but the air stopped my breath and I was forced to gang.'

Six years old Margaret Leveston carried loads that weighed fifty six pounds.

'Been down at coal-carrying six weeks, make ten to fourteen rakes a day, the work is na guid it is so very sair. I work with sister Jessie and mother; dinna ken the time we gang. It is gai dark.'

Margaret Drylie, sixteen years old worked for four years wheeling coal below ground either from five in the morning to four, or from six at night to four in the morning, sometimes working double shifts. Work, she said was 'sore straining, was laid off three months with pain in limbs from overwork.'

Ellison Jack, eleven years old , told how she had been working below 'three years on my father's account; he takes me down at two in the morning and I come up at one and two the next afternoon. I go to bed at six at night to be ready for work next morning. I have to bear my burthen up four traps, or ladders, before I get to the main road which leads to the pit bottom.'

This journey had to be done twenty times to fill her allotted five tubs, each holding four and a quarter hundredweights, and Ellison was beaten with a strap if she failed to fulfil her quota.

Robert Franks, the member of the Royal Commission who collected evidence   in Fife and the Lothians, prepared the following report:

'A brief description of this child's workplace will better illustrate her evidence.

Turnpike stair

She has first to descend a nine-ladder pit to the first rest to where a shaft has been sunk to draw up baskets or tubs of coal. She then takes her creel (a basket formed to the back, not unlike a cockle shell, flattened towards the neck so as to allow lumps of coal to rest on the back of the neck and shoulders) and pursues her journey to the coal face. She then lays down her basket, into which the coal is rolled and it is frequently more than one man can do to lift the burden on her back. The tugs or straps are placed over the forehead and the body bent in a semi-circular form, in order to stiffen the arch. Lumps of coal are then placed on the neck, and she commences her journey with her burden to the pit bottom, first hanging her lamp to the cloth crossing her head.

In this girl's case, she has first to travel about fourteen fathoms (twenty eight metres) from coal face to the first ladder which is about eighteen feet high and so on to the third and fourth ladders till she reaches the pit bottom. The height ascended and the distance along the roads added together, exceed the height of St. Paul's Cathedral and it not infrequently happens that the tugs break and the load falls on the females who are following. However incredible it may appear, yet I have taken evidence from fathers who have ruptured themselves from straining to lift coal on to their children's backs'.

Some estimate of the height to be climbed can be made from this illustration from the CEC

CHAPTER FOUR

WOMEN'S VOICES.

Robert Franks was a conscientious investigator. While other commissioners recorded around fifty interviews each, he visited over one hundred collieries in Fife, Clackmannanshire, Stirling and the Lothians and interviewed four hundred and twenty nine people, most of them children, and found that about a quarter of all mine workers were under thirteen years of age.

In order to achieve a picture of the social, educational and spiritual condition of the people, he spoke to mine-owners, ministers and teachers and visited women in their homes. These he described as one roomed hovels, about ten to twelve feet square, being home to families with up to ten children and shared with a collection of lodgers, fowls, dogs, occasionally a jackass and other animals. Furniture consisted of one or two dilapidated beds, a few stools or stones to sit on and some damaged crockery. The lack of furniture was seen as an advantage by the miner for, if he had to move, there were no great flitting costs. All household waste was deposited outside the door, drainage and sanitation being non-existent, as were home comforts of any kind because no-one had time or energy to enjoy such a thing. All women's energies were taken up with working and perpetual childbearing as the women in the following interviews, taken from Frank's report explain.

Jane Johnson:
'I was seven and a half years of age when my uncle yoked me to the pit as father and mother were both dead. I could carry two hundredweights when fifteen but now feel the weakness upon me from the strains. I have been married ten years and had four children, have usually wrought till one or two days of birth. Many women get injured in back and legs and I was crushed by a stone some time since and forced to lose one of my fingers'.

Isabel Hogg, fifty three, retired coal bearer:
'Been married thirty seven years; it was the practice to marry early, when the coals were all carried on women's backs, men needed us. I have four daughters married and all work below till they bear their bairns. One is very badly now from working while pregnant which brought on a miscarriage from which she is not expected to recover. Collier people suffer much more than others - my guid man died nine years since with bad breath, he lingered some years but was entirely off work eleven years before he died'.
Jane Peacock Watson, age forty, coal bearer:

'I have wrought in the bowels of the earth thirty three years; have been married twenty three years and had nine children; six are alive, three died of typhus a few years since, have had two dead born, think they were so from oppressive work; a vast women have dead births...... I have always been obliged to work below till forced to go home to bear the bairn, and so have all the other women. We return as soon as we are able, never longer than ten or twelve days, many less if we are needed.'

Catherine Kerr, 35, putter:
'Work below ground with husband, have four children, the youngest seven months, went below after its birth as husband is short of breath.'

Elizabeth Mc Neil, 38:
' I knew a woman who came up and the child was born in the field next the coal hill. Women frequently miscarry below and suffer much after. Vast of women are confined before they have time to change themselves.'
 One woman said that the chain didn't trouble her too much between the legs when she was in the family way because she always gave up work after the fifth month. The mining foreman of Ormiston Colliery said that 'In fact women always did the lifting, or heavy part of the work and neither they nor the children were treated like human beings where they are employed. Females submit to work in places where no man or even lad could be got to labour in; they work in bad roads, up to their knees in water, their posture almost double. They are below till the last hour of pregnancy. They have swelled ankles and haunches and are prematurely brought to the grave or, what is worse, to a lingering existence.'
The mortality rate was appalling, the numbers of deaths in some areas greater than those of births. Babies, usually small and wasted, were taken down the pit and some fed only on mother's milk until the age of two. Others had no milk at all but were left in the care of childminders, who earned a pittance, fed their charges on coarse food which irritated their stomachs an then and pacified them with whisky, either neat or with warm water. Girls as young as eight looked after smaller siblings, many children suffered from respiratory diseases from the animals in the house and all were under nourished. Meat seldom formed part of their diet, which consisted mainly of porridge, oatcake and oat bread.
It is hardly surprising then that education in housewifery and child care normally passed from mother to daughter, was almost impossible in this situation. It is always unwise to generalise because of evidence that some girls supplemented their income with fine needlework - tambour work which consisted of delicate embroidered lace, sometimes on fine muslin - and with knitting, and made their own clothes without the benefit of formal teaching, But on the whole, commissioners found that girls had no instruction in housewifely arts. It was not to be wondered at, then, that 'Tradesmen scarcely ever marry colliers' daughters as they know nothing of housework. How in the name of reason could they? Are they to learn it in the pit?' Franks reported meeting 'respectable coal wives' with clean houses, but they were worthy of note simply by being exceptional.

The men who campaigned for laws to prevent women from working underground were aware that the welfare of miners and their children rested with the women, who themselves had no power to improve their lot. It was believed that the moral condition of the miner could be changed only by giving him a sober and decently educated female, not someone who had been 'degraded by brutal work in the pit.' Let her become a house wife and mother, they said, and all social ills would be solved. To many, it was the moral rather than the physical danger that threatened. A pamphlet, published in 1793, had described miners as being 'destitute of all principles of religion and morality, perfectly indifferent to the opinion of the world.....The manner of treating their wives and daughters, of making them bearers in the pits, of employing them to carry coal on their backs; of mixing the sexes in the pits, did not contribute to cultivate or humanise their manners.' [1]

Robert Bald was one of those who attempted to improve both the working and home conditions of mining families. A leading civil engineer, and a factor to the Earl of Mar, he hoped in his General View of the Coal Trade in Scotland, published in 1808 to arouse public indignation by describing 'the conditions of this class of women whose peculiar situation was but little known to the world.' He wrote of his meeting with one of these women:

'A married woman came forward, groaning under an excessive weight of coals, trembling in every nerve and almost unable to keep her knees from sinking under her. On coming up she said in a plaintive and melancholy voice, 'Oh, sir, this is sore, sore work. I wish to God the first woman who tried to bear coals had broke her back and none would have tried it again'.

Bald believed that the home life of his miners left much to be desired and that laziness and drunkenness was a result of this rather than the cause. His attempts to make improvements were misunderstood and unwelcome. Miners believed that the only results would be increased profits for the Earl of Mar, owner of the Alloa Coal Company, but Bald persisted. He hoped to increase the size of miners houses, to remove ashpits and to sweep the streets daily; he began lectures on Order and Cleanliness; circulated rules about cleaning and whitewashing and tried to ban the keeping of animals - pigs, poultry and dogs - in the houses. Inspectors were appointed to see these tasks were carried out and infuriated women locked the inspectors out and hurled abuse.

In 1832, thirty three people died of cholera and Bald blamed the high death toll on the practice of excessive whisky drinking at wakes. He tried to ban whisky and bought in 'a supply of moderate priced wine to be kept at the colliery change house' so that on mournful occasions friends could still have a refreshment without getting drunk. Baillies and watchmen were set to patrol the streets and report those found drunk and prayer meetings were begun to encourage men on to the path of temperance. The miners retaliated by staying away from work and Bald eventually had to resign his post as factor .However, he went on to support the Earl of Shaftesbury in his campaign which eventually resulted in the prohibition of women being employed in any coal mine in the country. In addition, because of Bald's influence, the Earl of Mar banned females from working underground in the 1830s. It was estimated that women carried fifty thousand tons of coal out of Mar's pits each year and one fifth of his mining labour force was under thirteen years of age.[2]

One paragraph in the Commission's report claimed that 'in districts in which females are taken down into the coal mines, both sexes are employed together in precisely the same kind of labour, and work for the same number of hours; that the young girls and boys, and the young men and women, and even married women and women with child, commonly work almost naked, and the men, in many mines, quite naked; all classes of witnesses bear testimony to the demoralising influence of the employment of females underground.'

Engels claimed that the number of illegitimate children born to miners was disproportionately large and indicated what went on among 'the half savage population below ground'.[3] Women it seems, were doubly at fault. They failed their men by being unable to provide a comfortable home and were an evil influence in the workplace. In an age when voluminous clothes were worn, the glimpse of an ankle seen as shocking, and grand pianos had frills to hide their naked legs, it is hardly surprising that women working half naked would be seen as a greater offence than their being forced to work as pack horses.

Moral problems were high on the reformers' agenda but it is accepted now that many claims of moral degeneracy were based on ignorance. Middle class investigators had no understanding of different life styles. Even Lord Ashley, in a speech to Parliament, spoke of girls being " insulted, oppressed and even corrupted,"[4] when in fact, many girls worked in family groups or with close relatives and would be protected by them.

CHAPTER FIVE

AFTER THE ACT

By 1842, it was obvious that reforms in mining would not come from within. Reform was seen as destroying the economic basis of the coal industry which was in effect, getting maximum profit from minimum investment. The general complaint was that if women and children were banned from working underground, costly improvements would have to be made to enable men to do the same job. Owners, it was said, would be compelled to alter their systems, ventilate better and make better roads so men 'who now work three or four days will be encouraged to work for themselves.' [1] When wives and children were involved men tended to work, at the most, nine days in a fortnight but in female-free pits, they had to work eleven or twelve days. Yet no-one thought it odd that men were not expected to accept working conditions which women had, for years, been forced to endure. Proposals to replace women bearers with ponies - surely a tacit admission of the role women played - were turned down because of the expense involved. Some owners objected to what they saw as undue interference in the way they ran their business and threatened with ruin others who tried to improve working conditions in their own mines.

The horrors unleashed by the Commission, however, had caused such a wave of revulsion in the country that Parliament had no difficulty passing an act in 1842, [2]

Working half naked was seen as more disgraceful than being used as a human carthorse

banning all females from working underground, in spite of considerable opposition from both owners and workers. Land and mine owners saw their royalties and profits disappearing and workers saw their already abysmal standard of living being reduced even further. There were no statistics available so the numbers involved in the country as a whole were vastly overrated, but the extent of the problem within areas where women and children traditionally made up a substantial part of the work force was enormous. Mining families were, by and large, totally dependent on the labour of women and children and were bitterly opposed to reform which would rob them of their livelihood. After the bill was passed, some owners tried to have it repealed by exploiting the grievances of women who had been put out of work. The Marquess of Londonderry, whose family fortunes were based on exploitation of the miners, fiercely opposed it in the Lords, claiming it would prevent the working of many of the most important mines in the country.

By the 1842 Mines and Collieries Act all females and children under the age of ten were banned from working underground; but until new working practices increased output, a large part of the family's wage earning capacity disappeared so improvements of one kind were undermined by an increase in economic hardship. Shaftesbury and his supporters saw only the evils inherent in the existing situation, and either ignored or were unaware of the reality of the new situation. The idea behind the ban was not that women should find other employment, but would stay at home. Girls would be educated in domestic economy but this would take from one to two years because 'they are totally unfit for other occupations.' They would be taught separately from boys, given education appropriate to domestic service which was seen as the ideal. Industrial schools would train women for 'the duties of housekeeping, the arts of cooking, washing and sewing' and the result of this would be the beneficial effects on their men folk who would become sober, steady workmen who would work longer and produce more coal.

The proper job for a woman, it was believed, was to attend to a mother's and housewife's duties. A woman who worked was 'an affront against nature and the protective instinct of a man.' But women banned from the pits could not afford to stay at home and in any case, large numbers of those employed were young unmarried women. In the East of Scotland, there were approximately two and a half thousand women in the mines, and little or no other industry in the area. In addition, the traditional suspicion of mining communities remained and the women themselves felt that they were accustomed to mine work, knew no other trade and were fit for nothing else. They could not compete for jobs with women from different backgrounds.

In the years following the passing of the act, a number of petitions were presented to Parliament and the suspicious might detect traces of influence from the mine owners whose interest was in retaining a cheap and malleable work force. One petition from Newbattle attacked the 'falsehoods, exaggerations and antipathies' of the report, complaining that instead of being compared with other workers they were compared to 'perfection itself' so it was obvious that they would be found wanting.[3]

In Dunfermline, seventy three women from Townhill petitioned Parliament claiming that the nature of their work precluded them from training as domestic servants or outdoor labourers.[4]

As well as being made redundant, widows or single women caring for elderly dependants also faced losing their homes which were tied to colliery working. At Wellwood Colliery nineteen out of the eighty women who lost their jobs supported relatives and at Fordell, thirty four women had the responsibility for sixty three people. The problem of finding employment was exacerbated by the sheer numbers involved. One hundred and forty seven women had to leave the Alloa collieries, one hundred and five went from Clackmannan, and one hundred and twenty six from the Carron company's pits at Stirling. Many of these women had only worked in the pits because no other jobs were available. A few women found work in brick works or in agriculture and domestic service provided another kind of slavery for a few others. There was no parish relief so women were sometimes reduced to pitiable and humiliating employment such as hawking or collecting manure from the roads. The MP for Renfrew received a deputation of pit women and their husbands who explained that they were ' in a state of great destitution, they were deprived of an employment with which they were perfectly satisfied, and were reduced to a state of idleness and misery'.[5] It is hardly surprising , then, that miners continued to allow their wives and children to go on working underground.

At some Scottish pits, men were sacked from the pit head and their jobs given to women. The reason given was that men would more easily find alternative jobs but women were expected to do the same job for less money and so were accused of directly competing with men for the work available and providing cheap labour. The women had no choice but to accept what was offered. This, in turn, led the newly formed miners unions to support female exclusion from all pit work, and to claim that mining was not suitable employment for women. The owners' view was that as well as being cheaper, women were not allowed to be union members so were therefore less likely to make trouble.

Initially the Bill had sought to forbid women from entering mines at all but this was amended to allow them access providing they were not employed there. This amendment made the act difficult to enforce. With one inspector to cover all two thousand pits in the country, it was an impossible task so it was simple, as well as being in the owner's economic interest to ignore the law. In some places, women who tried to go down the pit were driven back by stones but usually they continued to work underground and overseers turned a blind eye. In Midlothian women disguised themselves as men and were taken to court in Edinburgh but dismissed with a promise not to repeat the offence. A letter from the Secretary of Scottish miners in 1844 reported that "the act for prevention of females working in pits is daily and openly violated. The Clackmannan Coal company, trading under the name of Wilson and Company employ upwards of one hundred females in their coal works in this neighbourhood without the least attempt at concealment." The letter also claimed that women were still employed in coal pits in other parts of Scotland, many at the Duke of Hamilton's collieries near Falkirk. Three years after the Mines Act, the law was a 'dead letter.' If not deliberately broken, it was very conveniently bent.

On November 1,1842, the following notice had appeared at Redding Colliery:

> In consequence of the Act 1842 the Duke of Hamilton hereby intimates, that from and after the 10th November no Females, under 18 years of age, nor after the 1st of March next year, shall any Females, of whatever age, be employed in the underground operations at Redding Colliery. He farther intimates, that from and after the 1st day of March next, no male persons under the age of 10 years, shall be employed underground at said Colliery; and he strictly prohibits all his Colliers and Workmen, at said Colliery, from, in any way taking the assistance of any such in the underground operations which are being performed by them.
>
>   (signed)
>   JOHN JOHNSTON
>   Manager

Another, three years later, showed how little attention was being paid to the law. [6]

> **NOTICE**
> **NO FEMALES**
>
> **Permitted, on any account, to work under ground at this colliery; and all such is STRICTLY PROHIBITED, by Orders from His Grace, the Duke of Hamilton.**
>
> **JOHN JOHNSTON, Overseer**
>
> **Redding Colliery: 4th March 1845**

Having these notices displayed prominently was sometimes seen as complying with the act. Women were forbidden. It said so on the notice, so nothing more needed to be done by way of enforcement.

The Chartist newspaper, *The Northern Star*, supported the miners demand for higher wages and saw the removal of women from mines as one way of achieving this, but the coal masters were adept at breaking the law. The Duke of Hamilton was singled out for special mention because of his position as the principal nobleman in Scotland, the lord lieutenant and the Queen's representative , and because of the way he totally ignored the laws of the land except where it suited him. A number of pits in the Dunfermline area were evading the law, though information was lodged against them. The colliery managers insisted that no laws were being broken, and in spite of evidence the Fiscal and even the Lord Advocate upheld their claim. The Fiscal was personally connected with several of the local collieries.

In 1846 a report of the death of three women in a mining accident demonstrated that the law was not working. Twenty years later, in 1866, an inquest on a woman killed in a Welsh pit said she was thirty five and pregnant. [7] Everyone knew the laws were being flouted and women still worked below ground but the mine agents claimed that dressed in trousers, rough jackets, boots and flat caps it was impossible to distinguish women from men without a close investigation.

In 1865, Arthur Joseph Munby, a London barrister and staunch supporter of women's right to work interviewed a thirty seven year old pit head worker. She had been in service but left to go down the pit, seven years after it had been made illegal. Dressed as a man. she drew wagons or 'corves' with a belt around her body and a chain between her legs, and claimed that her breeches kept the chain from hurting. She went on hands and feet 'like a horse' and because there were no rails, was often 'over my wrists in mud.' She worked below for a month before being found out and sent to work at the pit head. There were probably many more who went unrecorded. [8]

The first mines inspector never went underground and moreover, gave notice of impending visits. Coal owners could be fined for employing women but fines were small and easily affordable and illegal workers could be paid lower wages. In some pits four pence was kept off women's pay to pay for possible fines. In the Stirling area in 1848, girls started work underground for the first time, but at the Carron works, the pit was stopped every time a woman was found in the mine. [9] This punished everyone for the actions of the few and because they were losing money , it was in the miners' interest to adhere to the law. The practice stopped eventually because of the publicity given to accidents, and because the miners themselves realised that the employment of women could be seen as perpetuating low wages. The idea that a man should be able to earn enough to keep his family was gaining ground and in 1848, Lochgelly miners took proceedings against the coal master for employing women. [10]

Though banned from underground working, many women continued to work on the surface, mostly separating stones and dirt from coal at the pit head .For more than fifty years determined but unsuccessful efforts were made to oust them.

Sligo Street Cowdenbeath

Typical rows of miners houses in Cowdenbeath.

CHAPTER SIX

MONEY AND MORALS

Any nineteenth century discussion of morals related only to the workers and to the shocking situation of partly clothed men and women working in close proximity. Many complaints of immorality rose from the ignorance of people with no first hand experience of mines or mining, and no understanding of a way of life alien to their own. Engels wrote about the 'half savage population underground'[1] but most miners worked in family groups and girls were in more danger of a beating from their fathers than of indulging in sexual misconduct. Carrying several tons of coal a day would leave little time or inclination for such indulgence but newspapers concentrated on the proximity of the sexes, showing a morbid curiosity and a fascination with details of women's dress, which appealed to the prurience of comfortable middle classes. Girls were 'dressed in boys clothes and as black as a tinker.' They had to draw loaded trucks by means of a chain which ' passing high up between the legs, had worn large holes in their trousers and any sight more disgustingly indecent or revolting can scarcely be imagined. No brothel could beat it.'[2]

A further cause for complaint by middle class observers, the lack of education and religious knowledge, again demonstrated a serious lack of understanding. For many miners, education was non-existent. Out of over three thousand interviewed only one hundred and fifty could write their names and only a couple of dozen could write a few consecutive sentences. Most parishes had schools but education was not compulsory and had to be paid for. Colliery children either went for a year or so or didn't go at all. Some teachers had college education or special training, others had few or no qualifications and taught only basic reading and writing. They were paid a salary according to the number of pupils and the fees paid generally provided them with 'a wretched living.' Girls generally were ignorant of knitting and needlework although these skills were considered to be universal. The nature and duration of their employment 'begets indifference to cleanliness and decent proprieties of home and person.'[3]

Some mine owners did provide facilities. The Elgin Colliery, which seemed to be the best managed in the country, had a school 'with two teachers who have free houses and coal. The men contribute to the school fund for instruction of children from five to ten years.'[4] Evening classes cost a penny, with the teacher being paid through the fund. Education, it was said had brought a beneficial change and a more sober set of workmen were not to be found. Many of the colliers were musical and between them subscribed twenty one shillings a week for instruction. Archibald Thomson, the teacher at Fordell School, had one hundred and seven day and one hundred and ten evening scholars including colliers, and had adult reading and writing classes. Other overseers, like William Fyffe, said, 'We have no school nor do we subscribe to one as the children are under the care of their parents who attend to their education and morals.'[5] Henry Cadell, of Torry of Inzievar Colliery said he had tried to establish a school but without success. Mary Hynd, aged thirteen said 'I dinna gang to the school as we have no good teacher. An old collier is teacher and wants five pence the fortnight which father will no pay.' [6]

Euphemia Japp, aged twelve, said she'd been at the coals since she was eight. 'I used to go to school but am too far gone to gang now. I sit at home after work and look about.' [7]

Jane Watson knew it was bad to keep bairns from school but women 'get so weak that they are forced to take the little ones down the pit'. [8] Even children of six did much to relieve the burden of women ruined by 'horse work' which crushed their haunches, bent their ankles and made them old women at forty. Besides, even if her children were inclined to go to school the nearest one was over two miles away, a fearful road in summer and much more so in winter.

Sunday Schools were not well attended. After working six fourteen hour days, it's hardly surprising that children preferred to spend a day in bed rather than in church or Sunday School. The catechism and principles of Christianity were taught but could have little relevance to these children. The Reverend Colin McCulloch reported that 'They have no pleasure in the broken education they are receiving, always at the foot of the class though head and shoulders above the others. They are awkward and out of countenance, most refuse to read and let their ignorance be known. I fully expect they will be, when a little older among the most disreputable of my parishioners.' [9]

Mr Ross of the Loanhead Coal Company claimed that 'in knowledge, both religious and intellectual, they are greatly inferior to all other classes, also in moral courage and enterprise and in taste for comfort etc.' [10] He went on to say that so deep rooted were their customs and prejudices that they didn't realise they were now free men and so continued the practice of arling.

The other major fault with miners was their fondness for drink and education was seen as a possible cure. One mine owner described them as 'a drunken, dissipated, improvident and dirty set of people with little or no notion of anything but drunkenness and rioting, laying up no provision for the future though in receipt of good wages which would be more if they worked six days instead of four. Wives are also drunken and children of eight to ten years old drink whisky.' [11]

He complained about landlords letting houses to people who convert them to places for the sale of liquor, thereby ' reducing the labouring poor to a state of destitution.'

Commissioner Franks included a survey of these drinking places in his report. Dalgety with a population of thirteen hundred had fifteen, the one hundred and seventy two people in Kennoway had thirteen licensed houses. In Beath one in every four houses was a pub and Ceres had twenty five inns and whisky shops. Henry Cadell complained that 'Drinking whisky and discontent are the two evils which prey upon the comfort and happiness of our colliers and if they were removed and they were educated, they might be as happy as princes.' [12]

Fine words, but how was this to be achieved? As early as 1790, Culross Colliery presented a different picture to other places, at least in the eyes of its owner, the ninth

Earl of Dundonald. Not only was his coal of superior quality but his colliers were 'sober, steady men of principle, well clothed, neat in their persons and well supplied with household furniture.' [13]

He ascribed this to the fact that their wives were exempted from the drudgery of coal bearing and by staying at home, contracted a habit of domestic attention and care of their families. His colliers were not paid their full wage weekly or fortnightly as was the usual practice. Instead they were paid sufficient to support their families and the balance was paid as a lump sum every three or four months. This unofficial banking system enabled them to buy clothes and household linen and to buy in a supply of beef in November. Their style of dress 'carried their taste for elegance farther than was thought necessary.' [14] They wore silk stockings on Sundays, and embroidered silk vests, with hair well dressed and powdered. Most houses had clocks and watches. The reason for the mutinous and disorderly conduct of most miners, he said was due to the practice of coal bearing women and to the fact that they were 'put like swine into miserable hovels.' [15]

A contemporary writer describes a collier village at Niddry Mill, near Edinburgh in 1854. It was 'a wretched assemblage of dingy low-roofed tile covered hovels inhabited by a race of men that still have about them the soil and stain of recent slavery.' The houses were chiefly remarkable 'for being all alike outside and in; all were equally dingy, dirty, naked and uncomfortable.' [16]

Oakbank looking west towards the bing, early 1900s.
Miserable conditions like these lasted well into the 20th century

These 'miserable hovels' had to be paid for; houses were tied but rent was deducted from miners' wages. There was no security of tenure. In 1837, when an attempt was made by miners in Colliershall in Lanarkshire to shorten their working day, the owners, afraid of the burgeoning Trade Union movement, reacted swiftly and viciously. They were well placed to resist demands because most families were living in dire poverty. Advertisements offering good rates of pay were aimed at Irish labourers and handloom weavers, who had seen their livelihood steadily eroded by the introduction of power looms, and were desperate for employment of any kind. An added incentive was the offer of free houses. In the same year, William Baird and Company, coal and iron masters, ordered all unionists to either leave the union or their houses. No known union man was allowed down any company pit.

In 1842, striking miners were dismissed on the fifteenth of one month and the new workers would have access to their houses on the nineteenth. In the same year, at Dundyvan Iron Works near Coatbridge, between three and four hundred men, women and children were evicted on Christmas Eve. There were widespread evictions during January and February when men went on strike to resist pay reductions. By mid-February, the colliers without homes or shelter were forced to return to work for a shilling a day less. Colliers were evicted from company houses in Coatbridge during strikes in 1847, 1856 and 1874. In that year, a large canvas tent, measuring twenty feet by ninety feet was erected to provide makeshift accommodation for one hundred and forty seven people. The Wishaw Press reported that evicted miners families, about one hundred and eighty individuals were camped out in a tent 'constructed of wood and covered with railway wagon covers'. [17]

In 1863 two miners were evicted from their homes. Their crime? They were selling a newspaper, *The British Miner*, which had been first published the year before. In spite of one family having a desperately ill child, neighbours were too frightened to take them in, knowing they'd suffer the same fate if help was offered. [18] In 1887, a wages dispute in West Lothian affected the whole shale mining district and lasted twenty one weeks. The Broxburn Oil Company threatened to evict one hundred and twenty one families. They claimed that, by striking, the miners had effectively left their employment and must therefore leave their homes. Some families left and their first attempt to build a wooden shed as a temporary home was stopped by Lord Cardross, who owned the land. Another makeshift shed, near Broxburn, held forty families. [19]

If a miner died, his family had to leave the house within fourteen days, unless there was someone to take over his job. Some owners prided themselves on the fact that they would not repossess a house while at least one child was available for work. Occasionally, where the house was so dilapidated that families had to seek shelter elsewhere, the rent still had to be paid.

Bad housing was not confined to mining areas. In the same way that child labour had been the norm in eighteenth and nineteenth century rural society so too were abominable living conditions - rat and vermin infested thatched cottages with floors of beaten earth and with no water or sanitation. What was barely acceptable in a

Living room of Lanarkshire miner's house. Redding 1930s

Bedroom of two apartment house. Standburn 1930s

scattered rural area, however, was intolerable in a concentrated urban situation Wherever a pit shaft appeared, houses of a kind grew round about it. With the upsurge in demand for coal and a steadily increasing work force, as many houses as possible were packed into a small area, with no attempt to provide roads or walkways.

Houses were one or sometimes two roomed jerry built shacks with floors of beaten earth or flat bricks. Kitchen furnishing consisted of a couple of beds in a recess. Fireplaces were primitive, ribs and a grating with sometimes a 'swey' to hang pots from. There was no sanitation and household waste and effluent was piled up outside. In Lochgelly this sewage was carried away in open ditches to the River Ore. Water came from wells or standpipes in the street. [20] There were no facilities for washing and few adults or children had the energy required to keep themselves and their homes clean. Health problems were linked as much with poor living conditions as the working environment. Doctors had no understanding of the underlying causes of ill health and though post mortem examinations were carried out, they did not link blackened lungs with coal dust. Because stone miners lived on average only two years, after starting work in the industry, the suggestion was that the stone exuded noxious vapours.

As late as 1927, an eminent scientist could claim that the inhalation of coal dust caused no danger to life but on the contrary provided protection against the development of tuberculosis. [21] The average life expectancy in collier villages was thirty four years and by the age of twenty few people were in perfect health. The nervous system, including the brain, was said to be so little used that colliers were 'more a mining or working animal than a thinking being.' Women had distortions of the spine and pelvis which made childbearing difficult, but in general their health was better than that of the men. They didn't work with stone, or hew coal and spent less time underground. The list of diseases is frightening and children died from measles, croup, diarrhoea and whooping cough as well as 'more serious' diseases like smallpox and typhus. They suffered from malnutrition and bad feeding from birth.

Margaret Johnson said that she wrapped her baby in a blanket and left him with an old woman who kept three or four other children, and fed them on whisky and water. Other causes of ill health were lack of hygiene and the requirement to work day and night. One commentator wrote that he had 'seldom walked or ridden through coal villages at any hour of the night, summer or winter, without seeing little boys and girls going to and from the collieries with their little lamps in hand or stuck in their caps.' [22] Sometimes they had bread and cheese to eat below but others had a meal when they got home. By then they were often too tired to eat or wash and they slept in their pit dirt. Most were small for their age and chronic diseases, like curvature of the spine, were common. [23]

The problems of drinking were eventually addressed by laws which prevented men being paid in or near public houses, though the law was still being flouted in 1860, and it was not till the development of the Gothenburg system that profits from the drink trade were used to provide amenities for mining villages. Until the Scottish

Education Act of 1872, which made elementary education compulsory for five to thirteen year olds, there was no law to prevent children being employed. When Franks asked coal proprietors and agents for suggestion for improving the moral and domestic situation of mining families, there was a certain similarity in the answers. Insist on attendance at church ; have an active missionary continually visiting them; establish weekday and Sunday Schools, because want of mental training causes vacant time to hang heavy; pay them monthly or only pay half wages weekly; have home visitors to make sure that houses are kept clean; keep children out of the mines till twelve years old - at present boys are taken down at six or seven to 'prevent them going wild about the town.' As happened with Bald's experiments in Alloa, any attempt to eliminate dirt and disease by enforced inspection and new standards of hygiene were greeted with hostility, and people simply refused to comply with what they saw as infringements on their private life.

A remarkable aspect of this discussion on morals was that no-one questioned the morality of coal owning dukes and lordships whose coffers swelled yearly while their workers slaved for a pittance and who kept these workers in economic bondage. One way of achieving this was by the method of payment. Some men received no money till the coal was sold, none had any control over their income and as well as having to supply one free load of coal a week, they were at the mercy of the overseers who could reduce or withhold payment because of the amount of dirt in the coal. The tally system which continued well into the twentieth century was a means of identifying the output of each man, but until miners were allowed to appoint their own check weigh man in 1860, there was no way of checking the accuracy of the weight or quality of coal brought up.

The dominance of coal owners over mining families gave not just the owners, but also the managers unlimited power. Though bondage had been legally banned it was still possible for a manager to insist that a man send his son to work in the mine. If unwilling to comply, he was threatened with the loss of his job and home without further notice. If a man was unable to pay his rent because of accident or illness, and provided he could guarantee his return to work, the arrears were allowed to accumulate and he had to pay one and a half times the weekly rent till the debt was cleared.

Mungo Mackay, the agent and general manager of the Lothian Coal Company, ruled the village of Newtongrange in Midlothian. A letter written by James Jarvie of the Blacksmiths Union in 1920 claimed that 'this is a village where the firm own all about the place - dwelling houses, picture house, public house, everything from the cradle to the grave. The general manager acts as the lord mayor.' If a man wanted a drink he had to buy it in the company pub. Miners who found apprenticeships for their sons, hoping for a better future for them, were threatened with eviction if the son refused to work for the coal company. One man, who stood up to Mackay and had to vacate his company house, was told that his parents would be evicted as well if they took him into their home. Men who were known to have been involved in strike activity could find themselves blacklisted and unable to get work in any colliery in million unemployed the choice between home and job or union membership was not difficult to make. [24]

Even in the 1940s, possibly up until the mines were nationalised, a man could be prevented from moving to another pit. Owners even made capital from any improvements that had to be made As one man put it, 'The coal owners were great at starting up bands and buying ambulances, but it all came from the men's wages. They paid for bands, street lighting, baths cap lamps, carbide, tools and explosives.' [25]

West of Scotland firms like Baird, and Merry and Cunningham had other weapons in their armoury which they used against their workmen. Over the years, they used unemployed weavers and displaced Irish agricultural labourers, but then stretched their net even wider. Scotland had a flourishing trade with Russia and Eastern Europe and mine and iron foundry owners in the west began sending recruiting agents to the Baltic. Lithuania was a farming nation, but agriculture had changed little over the centuries and most people lived on a subsistence level. A rise in population and increased grain prices led to a huge exodus of people looking for a better life. They were under the rule of the Tsar and opposition to this rule resulted in increased punitive measures against them. Books were banned and Lithuanian print forbidden. At the same time compulsory conscription into the Russian army could mean anything from three to twenty five years service. Small wonder then that offers of jobs digging coal were very tempting, especially as housing was part of the deal. Many saw this not just as a means of escape but as a stepping stone to America, though few made that final step.

What happened was that they found employment in coal mines, in the steel and iron works of Ayrshire and Lanarkshire, and were used as strike breakers and as a means of pushing down wages. Like the Irish before them, they accepted lower standards of working and living conditions, but because they spoke no English had no idea they were being exploited. In 1887 Keir Hardie and the Ayrshire Miners Union demanded their removal, claiming their presence was 'a threat to the health and morality of the place and is being used to reduce already too low wages.' [26] They were called Poles, forced to relinquish their names for others more easily pronounceable and on July 20th 1900, the Bellshill Speaker described them as 'a most barbarous people and in this district we seem to have the scum of their nation.' They were pilloried in newspapers for keeping lodgers and living in poor overcrowded houses in unacceptable conditions. The papers forbore to mention what contemporary accounts prove, that this was normal in Scottish mining areas, but hitherto had not been deemed worthy of mention.

What today would be called racism, was endemic. Offences which normally meant a fine of ten shillings could become fifty and transportation was often the result of a minor misdemeanour such as breach of the peace. No consideration was given to the wives and children who were stranded without a breadwinner and who often had to make their own way back to Lithuania in a fruitless search for husbands and fathers.

In spite of everything, by 1914 almost seven thousand Lithuanians were living and working in Scotland. They were adaptable and became good, dependable workers.

Scots and Lithuanian women at Carfin Brickworks c.1920

Lithuanian married women did not work and soon gained a reputation for their skill in sewing crochet and other crafts, but some of their daughters became pit head and brickwork employees. By 1915 a Lithuanian Working Women's association had been formed. On one occasion, during a boycott campaign against the Varpas Company in Bellshill for alleged war profiteering five Lithuanian women were arrested but released without charge. Later they formed their own co-operative society and the women survived by thrift and resourcefulness.

During World War One, many of their men were deported to Russia to enlist in the army and women and children were left suffering severe hardship. Neither Britain nor Russia accepted responsibility for their plight. Living in company houses and threatened with eviction, they were saved by the Lanarkshire Miners Union. Some found work in local brickworks or as surface workers in the mines. Others were reduced to stealing coal from wagons and potatoes and turnips from fields to feed their children. After 1918, only a small number of Lithuanian men were allowed to return to Scotland, because no sooner had the war ended than the Russian Revolution began. The families were dependent on state assistance and little was done to alleviate their suffering despite the efforts of people like John Maclean and other activists. The treasury decided to stop their allowances in March 1920 and women and children were 'repatriated'. This was a convenient way of removing the burden of their support and it also helped to ease the housing shortage. Strange as it seems, many families returned later and records show, that as aliens, every change of address had to be reported to the police. By 1939 there were still about two thousand Lithuanian families in the Central area of Scotland. Perhaps, after all, this is not so surprising. Travelling in Eastern Europe in the twenties, Jennie Lee wrote that she found a degree of poverty undreamed of by even the worst deprived mining areas in Scotland. During the second war, Lithuanian boys were conscripted into the British army or into mining and girls were assigned to war work away from home.

Another smaller group of immigrants were Spaniards who originally came to Scotland in boats bringing ore to Ayrshire ironworks. They worked for a time during the first war in the New Cumnock Collieries but moved on because of reports of higher wages in heavy munitions industries in Airdrie and Coatbridge. [27] Wage slavery was still alive and flourishing in the twentieth century. Though technically freed in 1799, another form of slavery - this time of debt - continued well into the twentieth century, enforced by the system that the Earl of Dundonald had fulminated against. This was the 'most injudicious and mean practice of the coal owners keeping a suttlery and paying the colliers to account of their wages in oatmeal, salt beef, herrings etc and last but not least Scots ale and whisky. In such trash the colliers wages are frequently spent before payday.' [28]

The truck or tommy system was seen, by those not involved, as having a great deal of virtue. A benevolent employer provided a house for his workers, gave them a shop where all the necessities of life could be bought cheaper than anywhere else and at the end of the month would give them the balance of their wages - if there was any thing left after all his debts had been paid. The Society for Bettering the Condition of the Poor said that 'the collier therefore is not able to squander the mass of his gains to the injury of himself and his family.'

One mine owner claimed that it was 'the responsibility of the firm towards its employees to see that they are well fed, well housed and that their children are well educated. I think that far more good can be done in that way than by workmen spending their wages to provide provisions for themselves.' [29]

Those who were involved saw it rather differently. They were at the mercy of the employer or his agent who had the power to fix prices as high as they chose. Truck is derived from the French word 'troquer' meaning to exchange or bargain but mining families had no bargaining power against what was basically mass robbery enforced on them by the coal owner. Truck involved paying men directly with goods in lieu of cash whereas with tommy, men got wages in cash but were forced to spend it in the company's store. Goods given on credit meant that by the end of the month men owed more than they earned. Drinking was encouraged because that meant that any wages paid were soon spent. Everything had to be bought from the mine shop which was either owned wholly by the coal owner or leased by him, usually to a relative. At Chapelhall, a truck shop manager died worth £10,000 which gives some indication of the profits made, even after the owner had been paid his share.

Independent traders were prevented from coming into an area. If a woman tried to buy goods elsewhere her husband was dismissed. Complaints of poor quality or short weight received similar treatment. Everything was trucked, from milk to whisky and Bibles. It was said that you could buy everything but your coffin in the company shop and in some places even this was possible. If the required article was out of stock, the buyer would be given a line to buy it elsewhere at the same price, with the owner's commission added. The school and the doctor, if they existed, were paid by truck and, if a man went on strike, the privileges of education and medicine were withdrawn. In any case, where a school was provided, the teachers' fees had to be paid whether or not your children attended school. Debts were charged at enormous rates of interest, from one to nine hundred per cent in some cases, and could be handed down to succeeding generations so there was little possibility of families being freed from penury.

Lawmakers eventually became convinced that this was wrong, as was the use of the truck shop as a barrier against men seeking alternate employment. They couldn't leave because they were permanently in debt. The Home Secretary of the time refused to set up an inquiry into the system, saying that restrictions couldn't be made without interfering with trade and that the remedy was a moral one, but those who expressed concern for the workers moral welfare were notoriously blind when it came to their own class. It was in areas where the truck shop system didn't exist that the foundations of the co-operative movement began which eventually would find its staunchest supporters in mining communities.

Several Truck Acts were passed, but early ones specifically excluded miners. As for later ones, owners quickly found loopholes or completely ignored them. For years after the truck system was outlawed, the practice continued. Wealth and social position combined to give owners complete immunity from prosecution. A Commons inquiry in 1871 found that the letter of the law was being adhered to if a man was paid in cash, even if he kept it only for the few moments it took for him to cross to the store man's office. A blacklist of 'slopers' was kept, that is men who did not turn over all their cash and they were either dismissed or refused further advances. A letter to the *British Miner* in 1863 refers to James Merry, mine owner and MP, as 'the great truck king of Scotland' who employed about a thousand men in coal and iron works. [30] Wages were paid monthly and, as the men were always in debt, they were forced to ask for advances. Merry was quite happy to do this as long as the money was spent in his shop. There were regular stoppages from men's pay - for rent, school, doctor, even for the blacksmith who sharpened the pit tools which, incidentally, the men had to provide for themselves. They were charged four shillings a month for coal, receiving less than they would have got from an independent coal merchant. Merry was a Member of Parliament, a legislator whose contempt for the law was obvious in the way he enforced the truck system in a country where it was illegal.

Two houses at Standburn, showing defective condition of roofs etc.

East Row, Standburn, looking north. 1930s

CHAPTER SEVEN

POLITICS AND PRUDERY

The Mines and Collieries Act of 1842 was passed because of the horror and revulsion which swept the country when descriptions of the working conditions of women and children in mines were made public. Many were genuinely shocked that they had for years supported agitation for the abolition of the slave trade abroad, while being unaware of the slavery in their midst. The 1842 Act was the forerunner of a series of attempts by government to restrict hours of work and to impose conditions regarding safety and welfare of both men and women. Women had no political or legal rights and were seen as requiring protection. Unfortunately, the men who made the laws were not always in the best position to judge what was best in the peculiar circumstances that prevailed. Nor did they give much consideration to the rights or desires of those they were legislating for. This point was put very succinctly by Hugh Miller in 1854 who said that this slavery 'seems not to have been derived from ancient times of general serfship but to have originated in comparatively modern acts of the Scottish parliament .... in which the poor, ignorant, subterranean men of the country were, of course, wholly unrepresented' and in decisions in the Court of Session 'in which no agent of theirs ever made appearance on their behalf.'

The state assumed responsibility for legislation against women working but did nothing to help them find alternative employment. The misery this produced was greater than the vice and immorality it was supposed to end. Women might find worse ways of earning a living, and by 1845, it was estimated that only two hundred and fifty out of over four thousand woman had found work.[1]

Those who returned to work illegally underground found it more difficult to do so after the appointment of mines inspectors in 1850, but records of accidents involving girls showed that the practice continued. After 1842, however, little concern was expressed for women and children working underground. The law had been passed, the practice was illegal, so it didn't happen. From then on, interest centred on what in Scotland was known as pit head workers. After a series of accidents when women fell down unprotected pit shafts, it was decided that this occupation, too, was too dangerous for women. But it wasn't the danger which most affected people's minds. Pit head working was 'contrary to nature, contrary to every sense of propriety and right, contrary to every law of civilisation, morality and religion.'[2]

The more reasonable view was that it was too heavy and hard, and in too severe an environment. Emily Faithfull was a publisher who made a life long commitment to the cause of women's employment, setting up her own publishing company to provide work for women compositors, and advocating women's right to paid employment. Speaking at the Social Sciences Congress in 1863, on the subject of employment unfit for women, she stressed that those who were trying to meet the wants of the new age and open new paths for women 'did not propose to encourage any kind of work which included anything intrinsically detrimental to distinctive womanhood. We do not want to turn women into men or see them doing men's work. But we go a step further, we do not want them to be beasts of burden or unthinking machines.' [3] Loading trucks, dragging coal wagons, carrying bricks or other heavy loads were among the tasks considered unsuitable. Twenty years later, after what she described as convincing evidence, she rescinded her opposition to women working at the pit head and began directing her efforts to help rather than hinder what she described as 'honest female workers.'

The same mind set which forced women out of employment but offered no other means of support continued to survive. The same arguments, based on the false assumption that women were still working *in* rather than at the mine, were put forward. In 1864 John Plummer was demanding that legislation must end this 'social evil' for the sake of 'generations yet unborn, for the sake of the future mothers of our mining population and for the sake of the moral, social and physical welfare of the present generation.' [4] 'Social evil' was a term used in polite society for prostitution but the mine workers' offence lay not so much in their sexual proclivities as in the way they dressed. Describing a visit to a Wigan pit, Plummer said he saw women with bared arms, one or two with short pipes in their mouths , performing labours totally unsuited to their sex. Degraded is a word that crops up continually in descriptions of workers, both in mining and its sister industry brick making. By working alongside young men, it was assumed that girls were constantly tempted into immorality, but a Select Committee on Mines in 1867 concluded that 'the allegations of indecency or immorality were not established by the evidence.' There was no call, therefore, to interfere with their employment.

Picking tables, Kirkford Pit 1913

Plummer saw the practice of women working at the pit head as a link to 'the barbaric past' and insisted on women's place being in the home, but that argument took no account of financial reality and even less of the actual truth of the matter. In comparison with working underground, girls working at the pit head had an easy time. The work continued to be incredibly laborious, but compared to other trades, their working conditions were not unreasonable. The list of occupations deemed suitable for working class women in Victorian Britain, and this included all girls over ten, makes horrifying reading. They worked in lead, copper and tin mines and in the quarries which supplied limestone for the Carron Iron Works during the Napoleonic Wars. [5]

Dressmakers and seamstresses worked eighteen to twenty hours in dusty, poorly lit garrets and the rate of sickness, blindness and death was very high. Women in the metal trades making chains, bolts and nails etc, worked in squalid domestic workshops. An 1865 Factory Inspector's report spoke of girls in brick works carrying ten to twenty pounds of clay in their arms, or twice that amount on their heads. For heavier loads they were 'harnessed to barrows like little donkeys.' In match factories, girls suffered from phosphorus poisoning, their lower jaws eaten away by fumes and their skin and clothes glowing with impregnated phosphorus. [6]

The 'unsexing and degrading work' at the pit head does not seem so bad compared to the glue factory girls who job was to scrape the putrid hoofs of sheep, cattle and horses. Cat flayers hunted cats and skinned them alive, bondagers or female serfs worked round the clock as field labourers and ballast diggers were paid a penny a ton to quarry clay and carry it to riversides ready for loading on ships. One said that she could only earn a shilling a day as 'twelve tons is as much as I can manage'. [7] Women continued to work till the onset of labour and returned to work within days. Not till 1891 did it become illegal to employ a woman within four weeks after childbirth.

At the same time, women were trying to fight their way into the professions. Over the thirty years before 1851 the number of women rose from three hundred thousand to over a million. Women greatly outnumbered men in the general population and, because there were not enough marriageable men, these women were regarded as redundant, surplus to requirements. Working class women did not have fathers or brothers able to support them in idleness like their richer country women, or to provide them with an education. They needed to work. But miners who had objected to the exclusion of women now took up the battle cry of unsuitability.

An article in The Colliery Guardian in 1863 said that they would be very glad if there were no young women working on pit brows provided they 'could find a more eligible way of earning a living but we would rather see them attired in patched trousers and old jackets and engaged in pushing coal trams than we would see them doomed to idleness.' [8] It went on to suggest that instead of waiting for an act of Parliament to bring this about, miners themselves should undertake to keep their daughters away. The miners' objections were based ostensibly on moral ground but in reality it was economic reasons that drove them. Women were beginning to be seen as rivals in the labour market. In the 1880s Scottish pit workers were earning only 1/4 or 1/6 a day and at no time were their wages more than two thirds of their male counterparts, even when doing exactly the same jobs.

In no industry were women considered equal to men, their work was seen as peripheral, as pin money rather than income and their working career, such as it was, would end with marriage. The argument used by some coal owners to exclude women in 1842 had been that a woman's place was in the home. Because their wages were seen as supplementary to those of the family's main earner, this was used now as justification for the payment of lower rates. As in earlier years, owners saw no reason for concern and felt no responsibility for women in their employment.

In the summer of 1879, Lanarkshire miners were said to be working for a shilling a day. A Hamilton mine owner defended himself against a charge of employing women after nine at night, contrary to the 1872 act by saying he was paying miners so small a wage they couldn't support their families on it. It was therefore in the interests of both miners and their wives that their masters were furnishing employment for women at fifteen pence a day . Women who had been working all day continued till one in the morning because by doing so, their day's pay increased to half a crown. [9]

The banning of women would hit owners financially because men would have to be paid almost twice as much, so it became expedient for them to support female labour. It also suited them to drive a wedge between different sections of the work force. Men didn't see women as possible partners in the fight against exploitation. Unions as a rule were not open to women and they supported demands for an end to female labour, though their members were not unanimous.

The 1872 Coal Mines Act fixed the minimum age of ten years for girls on the pit head, though the Education Act of the same year made schooling compulsory for five to thirteen year olds, and this law remained in place till 1887 when the minimum working age was raised to twelve. It also made clear the original intention of the 1842 Act that no woman be allowed to work or to be *in* a mine. Working hours, which had been fixed at twelve, were now limited from nine till five on weekdays, nine till two on Saturdays and no work was to be done on Sundays or at night. Meal times were also set, but as time went on, women ended up working longer hours because time taken for meals was tacked on to the end of the day ; in 1872 girls were still being employed on night work.

Women did a variety of jobs on the pit head, they worked with the check weigh man, checking tallies, operated points to direct wagons on different rails, drew full hutches from the cages and replaced them with empty ones, emptied wagons or tubs into the tumblers and carried wooden pit props from the yard to the pit shaft. Most, however, were employed on the picking tables, removing stones and dirt from the coal as it passed along the conveyor belt. By the end of the century most mines were producing several thousand tons of coal per week and it all had to be inspected. The various qualities of coal had differing uses but all contained varying amounts of 'impurities', and women might handle a ton of dirt a day. The work is described in detail in later chapters of this book by women whose memories of its hardship are still fresh and clear; but it was not the severe conditions or the sheer backbreaking toil that exercised people's minds and made them think the work unsuitable for the gentler sex.

Reports of discussions in Parliament show misunderstandings about the nature of the work with references to conditions that applied before 1842. Critics applied their own standards and preconceptions to a lifestyle they knew nothing about. Much debate revolved around morality. In 1842, it was the idea of women working half clothed, in close proximity to men that revolted Victorian sensibilities. Now it was the style of their clothing rather than the lack of it that came in for most abuse. Women wore jackets, like men, which was seen as degrading and worse still, trousers which were 'a disgusting kind of male attire which tends to destroy all sense of decency.' [10]

According to the MP Alexander MacDonald, women pit workers dressed 'like ordinary females with heavy shoes, stockings, skirts, petticoats, jackets and mutches.' [11] Compared to fashionable dress which kept the legs invisible but the breast bare, pit girls in trousers were extremely modest, their clothes covering the whole of their bodies but whether in trousers or skirts, they were all tarred with the taint of immorality. There was little direct evidence of bad behaviour but women were 'begrimed with dust and placed in temptations that might lead to immorality.' [12] It was believed that the chance of a woman straying from the path of virtue was linked to her choice of occupation. The work environment and rough pit language would coarsen them so

Women pit head workers preparing to tip coal at Carden Colliery Fife, 1896

they'd be hardly distinguishable from men, and their rough and dirty appearance would lead to a lack of shame and the likelihood of indecent behaviour. Mill girls and domestic servants were seen as reaching a higher plane of existence because their work took place in the shelter of someone's home. When the number of illegitimate children in domestic service was seen to be higher than in other occupations, no blame was attached to the males of the household. Instead, pregnant maidservants proved that 'incontinence and immorality prevailed extensively in that class of domestic servant'. Critics also ignored the fact that as the century progressed, the number of pit head workers fell and very often mill and miner girls, and indeed maidservants, were members of the same family.

The arguments for and against pit head labour confused the girls ability to work with their right to do the work if they wanted. One Member of Parliament reckoned that their work was less fatiguing than that done by nurse girls carrying heavy babies and propelling rickety perambulators but the suggestion of female inspectors was turned down. Doubts were expressed about the possibility of finding females who were robust enough to travel long distances and brave bad weather. [13]

If MPs and unions had concentrated on the dangers involved in work at the pit head, their exclusion campaign might have worked, but the government's lack of concern was shown in a ruling by the House of Lords in 1867. This decreed that no compensation was necessary for accidents because 'the miner received his wages not only for his work but also to compensate him for the risk he ran.' In 1894, the House of Commons presented a humble address to the Duchess of York on the birth of a son, and sent a letter of condolence to the French government on the assassination of President Carnot. They expressed no condolences for the families of two hundred and seventy eight men killed at Albion Colliery in Glamorgan. [14]

At least one hundred and fourteen women died in pit accidents between 1852 and 1890, many by falling down unprotected pit shafts, and at least one of these women was pregnant. The East of Scotland was one of the most dangerous areas for shaft accidents. Bridget Mechan from Airdrie fell down the shaft with her tub, another fell backwards because the flooring at the pit top was loose and moved when she put her weight on it. Shafts were unfenced till the number of accidents forced owners to take safety measures and to obey the law about fencing shafts but accidents continued because these procedures were flouted. Jane Winning from Southfield No 1 Pit in Stirling died in 1880.[15]

Wagons constituted another danger and girls knocked down by runaway wagons included an eleven and a twelve year old. Machinery failed, scaffolding collapsed and ropes broke. A firedamp explosion at Oakley Colliery killed Marion Drysdale when she was struck by timber at the pit mouth. Four women died and five more were injured by flying bricks when a steam boiler burst at Fordell Colliery . [16]

Ages of those killed ranged from eleven to over sixty but the majority were between sixteen and twenty five. Females accounted for only a small minority of accidents but these were given greater publicity. There was no training or preparation for the work but some people suggested that women actually caused accidents because 'they do not possess the presence of mind that enables men to save themselves in cases of emergency.' [17] There was a higher rate of accidents where women wore skirts rather than trousers, with more likelihood of loose garments being caught in machinery. Working at the pit head was deemed to be more healthy than other occupations, especially mill work. In Fife, mill girls were sent to the pit head to recover from anaemia. Certainly they worked in the open air and the winds that blew through the picking tables helped counteract the effects of coal dust. Many girls, even in the 1930s, preferred the pit to domestic service, 'The hours were shorter, the pay was more and you could call your soul your own,' one explained. [18] At the end of the day girls were able to spend the free time in their own way.

Much publicity was given to pit head workers after 1874 when pictures of Lancashire pit brow women appeared for the first time in The Pictorial World. This illustrated magazine sparked off a bizarre interest and they were seen as curiosities, causing frissons of refined shock in London drawing rooms. Books were written depicting them as defemininised: 'They did not look like women--- as they stood together at the pit mouth.' They had 'faces as hard and brutal as the hardest of their collier brothers, husbands and sweethearts.' [19] The heroine of one becomes aware of her inadequacy and achieves the pinnacle of success by becoming a domestic servant.

Moral arguments were based on the belief that women's constitutions would suffer from the harshness of their employment and that future generations would be puny weaklings. As well as being 'unfeminine and rough', working women were also regarded as dangerous. The abundance of young, seemingly economically independent unmarried women was seen as a threat to marriage and society. In fact they were bolstering the finances of their families. Accounts by pit head workers of the thirties show that the habit of handing wages over to their mothers was still normal. There was no belief in the right to one's own hard earned cash and only a small fraction was expected as pocket money.

It is strange then that their fathers, or some of them at least, actively supported excluding them from gainful employment. The numbers who would be put out of work were not nearly so large as in 1842 and the employment situation was much better but for many the idea was that pit labour for women should be allowed to die out. In fact by 1886 the number of pit girls had dropped - to approximately six hundred in East Scotland and around forty in the West. In Parliament the argument was between the members with a monetary interest in constituencies with collieries employing women and those who didn't. The latter were not philanthropists concerned for women workers but with what they saw as unfair competition. They were unable to benefit from the cheap labour women provided.

Two members with a background in mining and trade unions, Alexander Macdonald and Thomas Burt had been elected in 1874 'in the working men's interest.' Both came from areas where pit women were not employed and were staunchly opposed to the practice continuing. They hoped that the 1886 Mines and Collieries Act would

put an end to the dispute once and for all; but it allowed women to continue working.
A deputation of Lancashire ' pit brow lassies' went to London but they didn't get a
chance to speak for themselves. Speakers claimed that they 'wished to earn a living in
a way that suited them best'. One Member of Parliament, carried away by his own
rhetoric and labouring under the misapprehension that married women were still
working *in* mines said that though the work 'may not be very pleasant or seemly for
women, it was not so unpleasant or unseemly as an empty stomach and a family of
starving children.' [20]

The women's movement opposed the bill, because it conflicted with their hopes for
women's political and legal equality in the future and sent a message to the Home
Secretary that 'it was unjust for Parliament in the election of which women have no
votes, to interfere with the right of women to work.'

The extent of members' ignorance was demonstrated ten years later when during a debate on the Eight Hour Bill, one referred to 'the exceedingly healthy and happy nature
of the miner's life.' No miner suffered from gout , he said as many mine owners and
members of Parliament did, and suggested some of his fellow sufferers take a short
holiday in the mines to cure their ailments. No doubt he'd have been at a loss to understand the number of miners who volunteered to fight in the Boer war, considering
they'd be better off in battle than living and dying in poverty at home.

Miners and women workers at Northrigg Colliery

CHAPTER EIGHT

HOMES AND HEALTH

In 1886, less than seven hundred females worked at Scottish pits. By the beginning of
the new century there were over two thousand with half of these in Lanarkshire alone.
A number of changes contributed to this: improvements in the quality and quantity
of coal produced; a sudden upsurge in the number of newly opened mines with deeper
shafts - by 1911, Fife alone had fifty nine pits operating with a total work force of
nearly thirty thousand and an output of around nine and a half million tons; an increasing market demand for a cleaner product meant that screening and hand picking
became more widespread and this was seen as suitable for women so numbers began to rise. In 1885, John Ronaldson, Inspector of Mines for the west of Scotland
said that there was no valid reason why the work should not be encouraged, because it
was healthier than factory work, was not too severe and was better paid than most
other jobs. [1] In six years the numbers of pit head girls in the west rose from seventy
seven to over three hundred and they were being employed for the first time in areas
where women's mine work was not traditional. Probably over six thousand were employed in Britain as a whole.

One cause for this increase was the collapse of various textile industries which forced
a large number of girls into the labour market. The Royal Commission on Labour, in-
vestigating the employment of women visited Blantyre in 1892. Several large factories and calico printing works had recently closed and only one calico weaving factory survived. The only other occupation offered was at the collieries, 'where conditions are such that the more respectable girls do not care to take work there.'

The investigator described conditions at the mine which had not improved over the
years. 'There being no regular path or outlet we had some difficulty in making our
way beneath the wagons and among the mounds of cinders, coke, etc to the place
where the women worked. We found over a dozen girls engaged in picking stones
and rubbish from coal as it comes up. No accommodation of any kind is provided for
them beyond the rickety sheds at the pit's mouth where they work in all weathers.
These sheds, which are neither wind-tight nor watertight, are set on a sort of scaffolding and are approached by precipitous ladders or stairs. The girls work from seven
to five with one hour and forty minutes off, which is divided between breakfast and
dinner. The wages begin at one and four pence and rise to one and sixpence per day
and they work five days in the week. The work is quite unskilled, and although constant, is not particularly heavy.

It is, however, extremely rough and dirty and the surroundings make it most unsuitable for women, especially for young girls. There is no supervision of any kind and
the women workers are, as a rule, exposed to rough and very objectionable compan-
ionship. The air was laden with smoke and coal dust, and the persons and clothes of
the girls were exceedingly dirty and unseemly. I had some conversation with several

of the girls, and in reply to my questions they replied they did not dislike the work, and in any case there was nothing else in Blantyre that they could turn their hands to. Several of the men engaged at the colliery expressed themselves very strongly to me regarding the employment of the women there, and what they termed its 'brutalising' effect on them. 'The employment of women as coal pickers is comparatively new in this district, but I was informed it is gradually extending. The manager at this colliery told me he was replacing the boys, who used to do this work, by women and girls, as he finds the latter so much steadier and more regular in their attendance. He also said that there were no instances of immorality among the women consequent on the conditions of their employment, but that they had necessarily to hear a great deal of rough language through their association with the men at their work.' [2]

In the East of Scotland, where female pit working was common, the picture was the same. Inspector Robert Mclaren reported that girls were gradually replacing boys on the picking tables because they were better workers and gave more value for money. He also reinforced the idea that there was no need to prohibit female workers on the grounds of hard work, long hours, unhealthiness of the occupation or in the interests of morality.

The work certainly was hard. Robert Holman, writing in 1957 provides a picture of the pit head worker at the turn of the century, going to work between five and six o'clock in the morning, summer or winter, fair weather or foul, wearing coarse heavy boots, originally meant for men and a short skirt of very rough material. Her age, he says "may be anything from fourteen to thirty, but the majority are eighteen to twenty. Her duties around the mine are many, and although she does not run the great risk of the underground worker, there is always danger to be feared amongst the machinery and the juxtaposition of the mine to her field of labour. Pulling the full hutches off the cage, taking off the pins, (pieces of leather or wood with various letters or marks indicating the men who filled the hutches), running them along to the different sidings, putting the empty ones back on the cage, picking stones from amongst the coal, carrying pit props, are some of the duties to be performed.

That the work is laborious is no doubt, each woman doing as much as would be required of a man. Often long after the miner has done his eight hours, up the pit and away home, the pit head girl is still working away, carrying props and loading them on the cage for the brushers. Late in the afternoon, she may be seen going home at the end of her day's work, tired and with the grim outlook of the next day's repetition, a sure reminder of her lot. At home there are a thousand and one things to be done......" [3]

Another writer, Kellogg Durland, an American who in 1901, spent some time in Kelty, working in the pit and lodging in a miner's house gives a very clear picture of the work and home life of the community. His description of the dress and occupations of the pit girls is similar to Holman's.

'There is something reminiscent of early days in the appearance of the pit-head girls with their high boots, short skirts encircled by a binding string to prevent their catching in the machinery, half protected by blackened aprons, and old soiled shawls tied snugly round their heads and falling loosely over their shoulders. After the first hour of work their faces are covered with the dust that ever blows fiercely through the sifting shed, stirred to angry restlessness by the powerful ventilating fan whose escaping puffs send eddying whorls outward from the shaft with every ascending cage. For the most part it is heavy work for the girls, pushing and jerking the heavy empty hutches, from track to track, hurrying them back to the cages, snibbling the wheels of the loaded ones, hopping nimbly between the moving tubs that look for all the world like miniature railway wagons, performing their work with tireless dexterity, keeping the whole place in a flutter from early morning till mid evening, when, according to a factory law that almost suggests a care for these girls, the work is left to those who are better able to perform it through the night.' [4]

Carden Colliery workers c1910

It is interesting to compare this somewhat flowery account to the stories of the women who were doing the same work thirty years later. Durland's middle-class attitudes shine through his prose. The girls of Kelty who work may be roughly grouped in four classes, he says: pit-head girls, those who go to the mills at Dunfermline or Kinross, girls who go into service; those who become dressmakers.

The latter consider themselves superior to the domestics, 'who in turn look down upon the mill hands, and at the bottom of the list are the pit-head girls, lowest paid servants of a great and wealthy company who slave for wages that vary from one shilling and two pence to one shilling and sixpence a day. The pit head atmosphere is the most demoralising atmosphere that can be found in a small village. Some few of the girls who come from good homes hold themselves aloof from the others, but as a class they are a sad lot.' [5]

Even worse off than the pit head lassies were the brick workers. Bricks were made from waste material from the pit so cost practically nothing to produce. They were used to line shafts and underground passageways. Conditions, working hours and rates of pay were worse in the brick yards than at the pit head. Girls worked in temperatures above one hundred and forty degrees Fahrenheit and the air was filled with the nauseating odour of warm oil.

'These girls' Durland writes, 'are perfect Amazons in point of strength They each handled five to six thousand bricks a day, and as green bricks are made heavy by the water in the soft clay, each weighs about twelve pounds. The girls lift them, one in each hand.... working at a speed that is bewildering to a novice. From early morning they work... never slackening their speed as the day advances.' [6]

The work, he says, is not so brutal as the pit head but the hours are longer and the girls themselves are 'of a slightly better type, they are full of fun and keen on a good time but, on the whole, their boisterousness does not descend to vulgarity.' Old attitudes die hard. No doubt there were some rough and ready females but they occur in every situation. Durland maintains that he is trying to present a clear, honest impression of an unprejudiced observer, but his view is biased by his own background and life experience. His account of the home life of pit head girls emphasises this.

'The most striking features of the home life were the totally different standards of good and bad, right and wrong, and the subjection of the women. To deal with the latter matter first, I was at first surprised, but gradually came to take as a matter of course the servitude of women. Their slavery to the men was almost universal throughout the district. The men were looked upon as the wage earners, and the lives of the women were given up to making them comfortable. Not once can I remember any of the women eating their meals with the men in our home. In some houses where the families were smaller and the tables larger it might have been possible for women to eat with the rest, but in our house to have made room for them would have meant crowding and cramping the men. Any suggestion of inconveniencing the workers would not have been tolerated at all. There were two big easy chairs in the kitchen (which was our common room) and if either of them chanced to be occupied by one of the girls or women when the men arrived it was instantly left for one of the men to drop into. It was a common thing for the men to demand that their pipes be filled by one of the women. I have seen a son of one-or-two-and twenty order his mother across the room to get his pipe which was on a shelf directly above his head a few inches out of his reach from the chair where he was sitting. All the time the men were at home the women would hover about ready to be instantly commanded for the most menial services'. [7]

When Durland questioned this slavery, he was told that devotion was a better word to describe it. There was no debating the severity of the girls working lives. After a day at the pit head or brick works, they were expected to help out at home, to be servants to the fathers and brothers whose working day was not any more severe than their own. Young girls were made to look on work as a duty that could not be shirked and the women never complained. Durland assumed it was because they knew no better, having no idea how other people lived.

Durland described the house where he lodged as 'a typical miner's house, one of a brick row with triangular roofs. There was a parlour and kitchen on the ground floor and an attic above. When we were all at home there was little spare room, as together family and boarders made up a company of fourteen.' [8] That didn't include six dogs and a cat. He slept in the attic with four others and the beds were used in rotation by men on different shifts. As a rule, eight to ten people shared a two roomed house and nineteen people occupied one with three rooms. Durland found it hard to understand why, in a country area, there was such a shortage of housing and why the owners could not supply the homes which were obviously required.

He was very careful not to convey any idea of squalor in Kelty, a comparatively new village, with many new, even if over-small houses, On the outskirts, he said , 'one comes upon small rows of neat self-contained houses with flower beds and grass plots before the doors, and having every appearance of cosiness.' [9] The Building Society put up houses on twenty three year mortgages for a deposit of fifteen to twenty percent. This was a time of comparative luxury for some mining families, but in any society there are those who rise and others who find it impossible. Wages were reasonably high and extra money was used to make their houses attractive with pictures and ornaments, and also with more expensive items like pianos and harmoniums.

Mining wages tended to fluctuate and went down oftener than up and Durland's cosy picture is not borne out in other places. In 1892, William Dixon and Company at Auchenraith in Lanarkshire built eighty three houses for his work force, forty two with one room, forty with two. There were no wash houses or coal cellars and drainage from 'hen-roost privies' - so called because you couldn't sit down - was by open sewer. [10] In 1905, a report about Townhill, Dunfermline's coal town, the author complained that 'while the town collected seven thousand pounds annually in royalties, the workers house resembled lairs and were devoid of any sanitary arrangements, apart from outdoor earth closets.' [11]

In 1912, the miners were fighting for a reasonable minimum wage but another struggle - to improve their living conditions - was taking place. As a result of a campaign to force attention on their housing conditions, a Royal Commission on Housing in Scotland was set up but it didn't report till 1918 and was not published in full till 1921. An investigation in 1917 by the Carnegie Dunfermline Trust said that the mining population had not entirely shaken off the moral traditions of serfdom. Research showed that death rates were higher in all age groups for one-roomed houses and female death rates exceeded those for men. A high proportion of women in the twenty to forty five age group died either of tuberculosis or puerperal fever. In one roomed houses, one fifth of all babies born died before their first birthday, many from whooping cough, measles and diphtheria. [12]

The Commissioners included Charles Augustus Carlow, the head of the Fife Coal Company. The Commission's findings were appalling. Mining areas were far worse than in the most wretched industrial areas of England. Excerpts from the report are a damning indictment of the men who made fortunes on the backs of miners and had no compunction in demanding payment for these hovels. From the descriptions given it is easy to see that conditions had not changed much since the Earl of Dundonald's account a century before.

'The Miners' Row of inferior class is often a dreary and featureless place, with houses, dismal in themselves, arranged in monotonous lines or in squares. The open spaces are encumbered with wash-houses, privies, etc., often out of repair, and in wet weather get churned up into a morass of semi-liquid mud, with little in the way of solidly constructed road or footpath - a fact which adds greatly to the burdens of the overwrought housewife.'

Wash day in Wemyss

The houses vary greatly in construction, but a large number are of two types. The older is either a 'single-end' or 'but-and-ben', according as it has one or two rooms. It has only one door, and the solid back wall is pierced only by the smallest of windows, if by any, so that through ventilation does not exist. Many of the older houses show the faults of their class – leaky roofs, damp walls, and uneven and broken floors - the last a source of particularly bitter complaint. In addition, there are faults not found outside mining communities, the chief being broken plaster and fissures in the walls, where 'subsidence' has been serious, while in the worst houses in the West of Scotland the only place for the storage of coals is below the bed. The impossibility of domestic cleanliness and order where this is the case needs no enforcement.' [13]

What a nightmare it was for the miner's wife living under these conditions, may be imagined from the following description:

'If the workers in a house are on different shifts, the task of the housewife is complicated by irregular meals and sleeping-hours. If the pit is a wet one, the miners' soaking clothes must be left at night by the kitchen fire; and as the kitchen is a sleeping apartment even where there are one or two other rooms, the steam and gas which are given off as the pit clothes dry are highly injurious to the children, who may be in one of the two large beds nearby. In the absence of baths at the pit head or in any save the newest houses, the miner on his return must take his bath in the scullery (if there is one), or in the inevitable publicity of the kitchen. With this accumulation of difficulties to contend with, the standard of cleanliness and neatness attained in many houses (though by no means in all) is a matter for genuine surprise and admiration. In the numerous cases, however, in which water has not been introduced into the houses but must be fetched from a standpipe at the end of the row, a high standard of cleanliness cannot be looked for.' [14]

Sanitary conditions were a menace rather than a benefit to the health of the miner and his family and it is surprising that diseases like typhus were not more widespread:

'A word must be said as to the nature of the outhouses which fill the intervals between the rows. Occasionally there is a properly constructed common washhouse, but in the older villages more often only such makeshift and ramshackle washhouses and coal-sheds as the miners have run up for themselves. But the chief of these unsightly structures are the privies. In the West of Scotland this often is a 'privy-midden', which has only in comparatively recent times been expelled from the cities and still unhappily retains its place in the mining villages. It is a large erection, open on one side, where ashes and all other household refuse are thrown in, and closed (though often not adequately closed) on the side which serves as latrine. It is the only sanitary convenience in many rows; and it is so impossible to keep clean, so foul-smelling, and so littered with filth of all sorts, that no decent woman can use it, while if the children do so, it is at grave risk to their health of body and mind. Another case, one degree less bad, is that of the range of separate privies -one for each three or four houses in the row. Here things may be better if they are well kept, but the difficulty of keeping them well is enormous; and often locks are forced, and doors may even be wrenched off. The last census showed that thousands of one-room houses continued to be occupied by families; that overcrowding reckoned even by the most moderate standard is practically universal in the one- and two-room houses.' [15]

The Commission singled out some area for special mention and expressed admiration for miners' wives:

'We have been in some of the worst of the miners rows with roads in wretched condition - no attempt on the part of local authorities to keep them under repair - in wet weather, mud often up to the ankles and with everything around looking sordid and tawdry. Yet in stopping at one or another of these hospitable houses for a cup of tea, we gazed around in wonder and admiration at the amount of beauty these housewives had by dint of hard work provided - furniture, floors, brass work, steel facings of fireplaces, all bright and shining with polish and labour.' [16]

The Commission estimated that the extent of overcrowding was such that over one hundred and twenty thousand houses were necessary to solve the problem but because the houses belonged to the coal owner, and there was no machinery to insist on improvements being made, little was done.

Another report in 1919 by the Sankey Commission, which had been set up to investigate the possibilities of state ownership of the mines disclosed a shocking picture of the state of the industry, of vast profits from low wages and the atrocious social and economic conditions of the miners. Evidence was also given of health, education, accidents and housing conditions.

Sankey said that 'There are houses in some districts that are a reproach to our civilisation. No judicial language is sufficiently strong or sufficiently severe to apply to their condemnation.'

Descriptions of miners rows in Lanarkshire repeated earlier reports of hovels without even rones to carry the water from roofs; coals kept under beds; no wash houses and water supplies from standpipes in the alleys. In West Lothian the only difference was in the colour of the bings which overhung the villages, red spent shale relieving the monotony of black coal. In 1914, The Scottish Shale Miners Association prepared a report which claimed that people were afraid that reform and betterment of conditions would lead to higher rates and more hardship. It went on to complain that the government could raise eighty million pounds annually for the army and navy to assist in destruction of life but was unable to find the half million which would assist in saving lives lost through bad housing conditions. They put forward well thought out plans for new houses - very basic by today's standards - to have an entrance hall, parlour, kitchen with two beds; scullery with cool pantry and coal cellar, a washing boiler and fireclay sink fitted on cast iron brackets; a bathroom with bath and wc; and a garden. The estimated cost including fencing was estimated at £175.00 which would be recouped in a very short time. [17]

Sankey recommended that one penny per ton should be levied and applied to improve the housing and amenities of the colliery districts. It condemned the existing system of ownership and suggested nationalisation but this was rejected by Lloyd George who was Prime Minister at the time. And again, nothing was done.

The 1931 census returns for Fife show over one thousand one-roomed houses, with seventeen of these having eight or more occupants; in Lumphinnans one had twenty four. In 1951, six hundred and ninety four houses had up to ten occupants, while two rooms held up to thirteen; by 1961 the number had risen to 733 with one house occupied by ten people. The question of sub standard housing only began to be solved when the local council took over responsibility for housing from the coal owners and in the forties and fifties there were still miners rows with outside toilets shared between two or more families. [18]

In 1944, areas inspected included Glencraig and Lumphinnans as well as Lanarkshire and Stirlingshire. The report said that 'there is no grouping of dwelling houses that can compare with collections of old miners rows, dreary long rows of single storey houses and between the only strips of drying green, though there is no grass left if there ever was any........Sometimes the atmosphere is polluted with noxious fumes from burning bings nearby. Many are unfit for human habitation and would be scheduled for demolition if alternative accommodation was available. They are in such poor condition that human beings should not be required to live in them.' [19]

In his autobiography, published in 1965, Abe Moffat wrote of 'houses built for fifty pounds over a hundred years ago. Miners continued to pay rent for these for three or four generations and some of them still exist. The only difference is that the dry lavatories have disappeared and lavatories installed but there are still no bathrooms.' Open gutters and privy middens were common in his youth and this 'showed the complete disregard on the part of employers and local authorities for the needs of human beings.' Miners were still looked on as sub human beings whose only purpose was to produce coat and profits for the owners. [20]

As part of the plans for nationalisation in 1947, the National Executive of the National Union of Mineworkers drew up a list of requirements which came to be known as the Miners Charter. Clause Ten demanded the buildings of new towns and villages of a high standard and 'situated at places calculated to enable miners to have increased opportunities for social facilities and to break down the segregation of mine workers and their families from the rest of the community, accompanied by the provision of adequate transport services at reasonable rates.'

Gradually the old miners rows began to disappear and were replaced by local authority housing schemes, but even as housing and living standards improved so the industry itself was deteriorating.

Women didn't spend all their time in the soup kitchens. Many can be seen in this crowd in the grounds of Glencraig Miners Institute 1926

A Workers International Relief Rally 1926

CHAPTER NINE

WOMEN, TRADES UNIONS AND SUFFRAGETTES

Though women were not allowed to join mining unions till 1897, their involvement in unions as a whole and in strikes began much earlier. Probably the first ever recorded women's strike was in Paisley in 1768. The Glasgow Journal reported that 'a female combination of this place, employed in the clipping of lawns, who refuse to work unless on higher wages.' [1] Presumably the lawn was of the cloth, rather than the grass variety. They were supported by crowds of journeymen weavers and others. In 1788 a sisterhood of spinsters stirred up their men folk to riot against the use of the newly invented spinning machines. They saw the development of spinning mills as the death knell of their own craft and the destruction of their livelihood. Spinning had always been women's work, that is where the term spinster comes from, but even in the spinning industry, employers protested that work turned out by women was inferior both in quality and quantity to what a man could produce. Lower wages for women could therefore be justified.

In 1823, women took part in a Luddite strike in Dunfermline and 'vied with the men in their efforts to destroy dwellings and looms'.[2] The following year, lace workers went on strike because their employer deducted money from their wages for the artificial light he had to provide so they could see to work. They were imprisoned for six months. In 1833, The Glasgow Spinners Association attempted, unsuccessfully, to negotiate equal pay rates with men.

In Wanlockhead in Ayrshire, miners had been given the right to build homes on nearby crofts, to keep cows and grow crops, although these crofts had no security of tenure and the income earned was used as an excuse to keep wages unreasonably low. When Ronald Crawford and Company leased the mines in 1756 and restricted these rights, the mines were visited by a lawless mob of women and men dressed in women's clothes who dismantled the windlasses 'and endeavoured by every species of annoyance to compel the company to give up their charge.' Only the removal of some miners by order of the Court of Session and the introduction of 'new and more tractable ones' dissolved the dispute. [3]

Though miners wives were not always directly involved in strikes, there were occasions when their presence was felt. Women were involved in demands for political reform, such as the Chartist movement, though in many areas only in support of their men folk. After the 1834 Reform Act, which triggered off a wave of resentment, because of its failure to accept the very reasonable demand by large sections of the population for political representation, the picture changed. In 1842, during a year of strikes, around two thousand miners including many from Stirling and Clackmannanshire attended a meeting in Dunfermline. A vote called for a nation wide strike and the implementation of The People's Charter, which included in its demands universal male suffrage and a secret ballot. [4] During another meeting at Clackmannan, a messenger at arms with five assistants, attempted to arrest a collier and was surrounded by a mob armed with sticks and stones. The windows in the local pub were smashed because the mob believed that the colliery manager had taken refuge there. A detachment of the 42nd Regiment from Stirling castle accompanied the sheriff the next day and seven men were arrested. The disturbance was said to be instigated by female colliers and Helen Yuill, described as the ring leader, was later jailed for eight months. Two companions in arms, Catharine Smith and Elizabeth Hunter were each given six months. The men all got lighter sentences. [5]

Miners and women pit head workers at Loganlea Colliery, Addiewell

At that time, women made up one third of the workforce of the Clackmannan Coal Company. Demand for the Charter dwindled but strikes continued. Miners in Lanarkshire had been on strike for two months and the owners of the Clyde Ironworks hired three men to instruct newcomers to the industry. When the men returned to their village to collect their families it was reported that 'they were met by a great crowd of women who began to call them Blacknebs, Clyde Blacknebs, and other opprobrious appellations and this continued for two hours.' [6] In 1868 another meeting of colliers wives resolved to assail 'infamous blacklegs' when they came home from the pit. In 1887, a wages dispute affected almost the whole of the West Lothian shale mining area. Teams of blackleg labour were so harassed by striking miners that they were afraid to leave their houses. The Blackburn Oil Company ordered one thousand men from their oil works to escort the 'blacknebs' to the mine. This procession was accompanied by a crowd of men, women and children ringing bells, rattling cans and tin trays and women stoning blacknebs coming off shift. [7]

Battles between miners unions and coal owners were always very one-sided. Miners had no cash reserves, they could be starved, evicted and have military force used against them. Vindictive owners and managers could order them out at a moment's notice and could cut off supplies of food, credit or even water. Men were dismissed for not being sufficiently subservient and so-called troublemakers were blacklisted . The landowners who made up the government regarded the slightest attempt by workers to protect themselves from exploitation as the first stage towards revolution. Fear of 'combinations', as early trades unions were called, resulted in

'the powers of the state being ranged against working men and women to quickly crush any infant trade union. After all, it was simple to sack the or-ganisers on the spot and make sure they were not employed anywhere else. It says much for the dedication and perseverance of early trade union organis-ers that any union ever came into being. It was not that early unions were ag-gressive or even necessarily seeking to improve the wages and conditions of work for their members. All too often they were called upon to plead that the wages and working conditions of their members should not be worsened.' [8]

Women went on strike at Nairn's linoleum factory in Kirkcaldy in 1870; at the Wallace factory in Perth the following year. Six hundred power loom weavers struck at Nithsdale in 1873 and eleven of their leaders were charged with breach of contract because they did not give a fortnight's notice of leaving their work. In 1875, one thousand women at the Baltic Jute Works in Glasgow ceased work, and nearly one hundred girls at a weaving factory went on strike because their lunch hour was cut by a half.

After 1842 there were, as we have seen, intermittent attempts to ban women from all work in the mining industry and this situation was ideally suited to the aspirations of the women's movement. There was a growing political interest among middle class women which burgeoned after the second reform bill of 1867. This bill gave more men the vote but again excluded women. People tend to think of the Suffrage Movement as being London based with all the action stemming from there but The Edinburgh Ladies Emancipation Society began in the 1830s and by the end of that decade several books had been written, calling for greater educational opportunities and more equitable laws. In 1843, Marion Reid's *A Plea For Women* was published demonstrating clearly why women had the right to choose who they should be gov-erned by and why there was no justifiable reason for withholding this right. By 1874 The National Society for Women's Suffrage formed branches in many parts of the country and Jane Taylour from Stranraer, the secretary of the Galloway branch from 1870 - 1873, travelled all over the country as far as the Orkney and Shetland islands making speeches in favour of women's right to vote.

The first women's trade union, The Women's Protective and Provident League was formed by Emma Paterson in 1874 ;its name was changed fifteen years later to the Women's Trade Union League. On a visit to America Emma had been impressed by the Umbrella Makers Union and used it as a model for her own organisation. The following year she was the first woman to be admitted as a delegate at the Trades Union Congress and she co-founded and edited The Women's Union Journal.

In the 1880s, the suffragist movement became involved in the rights of women to work. A wide ranging debate raised questions about the right of adult women to make choices on their own behalf. Only a quarter of all women were in paid employment at that time, but that was still a significant number. Protective legislation, such as the 1842 Act, was seen as helping those who were unable to help themselves but suffragists questioned the right of parliament to make decisions which in effect worsened the situation of large sections of the community. Women, they said, should be allowed to make their own decisions.

The trouble was that middle class women knew little about conditions of employment in any industry, and though they claimed to be working on behalf of all women, they had little notion of the lives and lifestyles of those they were championing.

One supporter wrote in her diary that she had purchased a photograph of a pit woman to remind her 'of the duty of educated women in defending the right to labour of the poor women.'[9] Suffragists opposed any regulation of factory or mine work, seeing it as an infringement of women's right to work but did not see the need for reform of working conditions or a reduction in the way women were exploited. It suited them to support the pit women because several attempts to pass a suffrage bill had failed and the Reform Bill of 1884 had upheld the right of any male, even one illiterate or cretinous, to have a vote. Educated women, however, doctors lawyers, teachers and women of substance, running their own or family estates were considered unfit to have any say in who was to govern them.

The suffragists clashed with the Trades Unions Conference, believing that men had no right to put women out of work. If unions were successful in banning women from pit heads, they believed men would then drive them from every trade and occupation they deemed suitable only for themselves. So pit head workers were being used as a test case. If the demand for exclusion were granted where would it end? However hard and unpleasant their work, they were a recognised part of the work force, and if they could be legally controlled or prevented from working, this would have some effect on other women's employment. New career opportunities were opening up ; between 1881 and 1891, there was a threefold increase in the numbers employed as clerks and secretaries. By 1911, though more professions were open to women, the higher ranks in teaching were closed to them, as were all ranks of the legal profession; though some qualified as doctors many hospitals would not employ them.

In coal mining, by the turn of the century, increases in mechanisation meant that fewer jobs were available for women and these were mostly on the picking tables. Improved travel facilities meant that women were no longer circumscribed by the job opportunities in their own neighbourhood, though in some mining areas, the prospect of finding alternative employment was practically nil.

Some support for both pit head workers and suffragists came from a small number of trade unionists, who believed that women ought have the right to judge for themselves what kind of work they should do. They feared also the possibility that if laws could be passed against grown women, the next step might be legislation against men. The pit girls, oddly enough received support from an unexpected quarter - the British Women's Temperance Association. [10] They hoped to enrol new members who would sign the pledge and remain good and sober citizens. Another group which spoke up in their favour was the Society for Promoting the Employment of Women. One of its Vice presidents was the Earl of Wemyss, of the same family as the man who claimed the right to keep his pits full of firedamp if he so chose. The Wemyss family had substantial mining interests, owning seven coal pits in Fife in 1911. The Society hoped to form a federation of groups to defend personal rights, and its members argued that the issue was one for women to decide.

Because of the suffrage support, it is perhaps not surprising that Fife had the highest number of suffragist societies in Scotland in the first years of the twentieth century. In 1907, their activity was at its height with meetings held in Dunfermline, Kirkcaldy, Kingseat, Cowdenbeath and Lochgelly. These meetings were attended and supported by miners. Arthur Balfour and Winston Churchill, who both later became prime minister, had seats in Scotland. Dundee was a safe Liberal seat but Churchill, who had lost the election in Manchester was booed when he appeared on polling day. A suffragist spokesman recorded her disgust that 'Scotland was a dumping ground for England's second hand goods.' [11]

The pit workers cause was taken up in earnest by suffragists who used slogans such as 'We claim the right to sell our labour even as our brothers.' This support was unwelcome in some quarters. The complaints about redundant women resurfaced

Jenny McCallum was blacklisted by Dunfermline linen factories for her suffragist activities

and Sir Almroth Wright, one of the most vocal opponents of the woman's movement wrote to The Times that 'The recruiting field for the militant suffragists is the million of our excess female population - the million that had better long ago have gone out to mate with its complement of men beyond the sea.' [12]

The Fife and Kinross Miners Association was formed in 1870, but women were not accepted in any mining union till 1897. The numbers of women members remained insignificant till the second half of World War One. Fourteen or fifteen local societies then had a membership of about ten thousand. This represented ninety two per cent of all pit head workers. Throughout the war, thousands of women worked at the pit head a large number as saw millers. An item in The West Lothian Courier reported in October 1915 that the United Collieries at Bathville, near Armadale, was employing two women, both wives of soldiers, in cutting pit props. By April 1916, men in various departments were being 'liberated' to join the colours and women were employed in the shale oil works as joiners, coopers and in the sheds . 'So far,' the report says, 'they are giving satisfaction in the several branches of work which they have taken up. With the probability of further men being withdrawn from the works in the district for military service, the employment of women on a more extensive scale is anticipated. While unsuitable for the main work about the mines, there are a great many operations in which they are capable of assisting, and no doubt their services will be taken advantage of as the occasion necessitates.' [13]

They were indeed taken advantage of. They stuffed bags with ammonium sulphate, filled oil drums, loaded wagons, and worked at the pit head tipping hutches. 'Women took over lots of jobs,' a contemporary report says, 'emptying the wagons and pulling the hutches, doing odd jobs on the bing and up the works, married women whose men were away in the army. Younger women, around eighteen years used to be on top of the wagons emptying them with shovels, pulling hutches out into the hopper and such like. Some even worked on the pit head along with the miners and had a hard time of it. They were resented because they showed they could do the job.' [14]

As the war progressed, the number of women workers increased rapidly as a result of the numbers of miners who enlisted and, in some places at least, the status of women workers improved considerably as contemporary reports show. One Stirling woman recalled how in 1914, 'The men were flying to the castle to register and they were short of young boys at the pit and they took on girls from fifteen. They had a head square and dark clothes and worked on a conveyor belt picking tones out of coal from seven till four. On dance nights in the Welfare Hall the girls would all be there and their hair shining. Folks will not believe that about the working class how clean and particular most of them were. The girls knitted for the Red cross, helmets and mitts and pullovers. Some of the men who came back were gassed and were no use.' [15]

Many girls began work at the pit head for purely economic reasons. 'I was in service with a vet and I left because the colliery was taking on lady workers and they were getting more money than in service - you got a pound a month and had to buy your uniform out of it. I worked first on the tables picking stones then went on to cleaning hutches. I got a job letting the men down the pit and I took their tools to the black-smiths to be sharpened. We flitted and I got a job lamp cleaning at Polmaise. You began to know each man by his lamp. I finished up on night shift, starting at nine thirty or so and I was there till all the lamps were given out in the morning at seven. Day shift was six or seven to four, back shift two till ten thirty. You carried your piece or ran home for something to eat. I enjoyed the job. I finished when the colliery closed for lady workers after the war.' [16]

Some women were permanent workers; others classed as substitutes, were taking the place of enlisted men on the understanding that the men would be reinstated at the end of hostilities. The agreement was that these replacement workers were to be paid men's wages but that didn't happen and they received only half of that entitlement. Among those who joined mining societies were five women from Wanlockhead. Apart from one reference to an Elizabeth Carmichael, who was employed washing ore at Lead-hills, there are no records of women working underground in lead mines until World War I one when thirty women were employed below ground. [17] Lanarkshire Miners Union had less than one hundred female members in 1914, and this rose to over two thousand in 1918. Men paid a shilling, women paid four pence and got strike pay in proportion, but were allowed no part in the management of the union. After the war, the number of women was reduced but wages were never more than two thirds and more often just one half of their male counterparts.

Pit head workers at Greenrigg Colliery 1920s

The Minimum Wage Act of 1912 applied only to underground work and though male surface workers eventually got an increase, the women didn't. The miners unions were in a quandary because although they had opposed women's work, women were union members and as such were entitled to union support. The Miners Unions compromised, reiterating their policy of doing away with women workers at the pit head 'owing to the conviction that their employment about collieries is not suitable.' Until that could be achieved, a sharp line was to be drawn under the kind of work women would be allowed to do.

But the pit head question was no longer seen as important. 1911 had seen the final attempt to end female pit working. In a period of high unemployment, the miners had fought for a minimum wage and their objection to women, especially married women, working was increasing. They were unsuccessful and a new Mines and Collieries Bill allowed all females over thirteen to remain at the surface. A proposal to stop future female recruitment was carried but was immediately rescinded and replaced with a measure to prevent injury. This forbade women to lift, carry or move anything 'so heavy as to be likely to cause injury.' Such a vague generalisation meant that it was impossible to enforce the law, and descriptions by women working in the thirties show how little it was heeded.

CHAPTER TEN

WOMEN IN POLITICS

The end of the war brought increased hardship but it also brought to the fore a number of strong minded women whose names may be scarcely known except in their
own locality but whose influence helped pave the way for the female councillors and
members of parliament we take for granted today. It also brought an increase in political activity and in many mining areas, especially in Fife, it was to Communism
that people turned. Nearly all female members of the party had mining connections,
through husbands, fathers or through their own work on the pit head. In 1920 over
one thousand girls were employed in mines scattered throughout the county and they
were the only group to join the Communist Party in significant numbers. Members
wives were targeted, rather than employed women because it was felt they would provide encouragement for husbands and sons, and were expected to vote as their husbands commanded. In 1934, a Lochore woman was beaten by her husband for
'unnecessary nuisance in the house since she joined the Communist Party.' [1]
Women were still seen as, and felt themselves to be, peripheral to the movement.
Meg Beveridge, the Cowdenbeath Party Organiser, left when her husband joined the
Labour party to avoid being blacklisted by the coal companies. One woman not afraid
to stand up for her principles was Elizabeth Watson, the wife of the Labour MP for
Dunfermline Burghs. Brought up in Cowdenbeath, she became a member of Beath
School Board in 1911, its Chairman in 1914 and served on Fife Education Committee
till 1930. She was closely associated with the Independent Labour Party, and was a
member of Cowdenbeath Nursing Association and of the War Pensions Committee.
Mrs Watson was eventually awarded an O.B.E but had resigned as a JP in Cowdenbeath on being requested to read The Riot Act, saying that it would be quite impossible for her to do so 'in order that the miners of Fife, my own class, should be shot
down by the military during an industrial crisis.' [2]
As soon as the mines returned to private control after the war, mine owners demanded a return to the pre-war rates of pay and from 1919 onwards there were strikes
almost every year, some of them small and local but devastating in their effects. In
1920, Bowhill Colliery in Fife was on strike for ten weeks. It was a time of massive
unemployment and the problem of those out of work was 'existing on less than half
the starvation wages one had got accustomed to.' [3] Children's health suffered, families had to give up their overcrowded homes and live in even more overcrowded conditions with parents and in-laws.
The Poor Law was totally inadequate to deal with a problem of such magnitude, but
the opinion of those responsible for dealing with it differed little from the whip and
brand mentality of the seventeenth century. Old prejudices, too, died hard. In the
1840s, ministers were scathing in their denunciation of the immoral, irreligious nature of their mining parishioners. In 1930, the Church of Scotland was trying to find

a new minister for the village of Cowie, in Stirlinshire. Cowie, according to report, was 'one of the most difficult places within the bounds of the presbytery and it was perfectly useless sending an ordinary man who simply wanted a move'. Cowie wanted 'a man with a crusading spirit who would recognise that he was going to a place in the front line of Romanism on one side and Paganism on the other.' [4]

Miners and their families were considered a feckless, irresponsible lot; cash payments would encourage drunkenness and reckless spending so food vouchers were given. Though the Shotts area recorded 'a remarkable increase in cases of malnutrition', they believed that there was no reason for a healthy adult - and adults in their reckoning included fourteen year old girls - to be without work, and surely starvation wages were better than no wages at all. Means Test Regulations were incredibly severe. Elderly or infirm parents were classed as lodgers and allowances cut; if a family had a lodger who paid more than four shillings a week , the wife was considered to be employed and so did not qualify for benefit. The Means Test added humiliation to poverty as every aspect of life was inspected. It was justifiably loathed. Parents who applied for boots for their children were told that they should go barefoot to receive the benefit of a free education. When children were fed at school , money was deducted from the family dole allowance because 'the child is not wholly dependent and is not being wholly maintained by its parents or guardians.' [5]

In Shotts, twenty six adults were fined ten shillings each and twelve juveniles were put on probation for digging coal from outcrop seams .Others were fined for stealing coal. Children foraged on bings and in places were reduced to collecting coal mud, the residue left by dross washing machines at the pit head. Coal gum as it was called, gave off a good heat. The Depression affected all British workers but few areas were as hard hit as the mining communities. Names like Jarrow have become a symbol of that age but many miners were among those who marched and in some quarters they received little sympathy. Men from Fife who went to London on a hunger march were arrested as wife deserters. They were found guilty at Dunfermline Sheriff Court but collections were organised and a successful appeal made against their conviction .[6]

There were local hunger marches, too, but in some areas, women marched in separate contingents and until the thirties no women were allowed to take part in any march which meant stopping overnight. That changed in 1933 when men and women who marched to Edinburgh slept in Princes Street. One of the leaders was Mrs Mary Stewart of Methilhill, who lay down on the tram lines in the morning, stopping the trams in an effort to find accommodation for the marchers. Red Maria, as she was sometimes known, came from Stoneyburn in West Lothian, one of a group of mining families who came to Fife after being evicted for their part in the 1926 strike. The family lived for a time in Lochore then moved to Methilhill, where she built up a reputation as an untiring worker. Never a day passed but she was at one office or another, dealing with unemployment, rent arrears and pensions. She was appointed as delegate to various committees of action and attended the Red International of Labour

Unions conferences and congresses. In 1933, when Henderson Stewart, the newly elected National Labour Party member for East Fife made a speech in favour of the Means Test, she proved that he could not calculate the scales in even the simplest cases. Even Assistance Board officers had to admit that they didn't realise how low the scales of payment were until they started operating them. It was not just mining families that were affected. Wages for government servants and the armed forces were lowered and the discontent in the Navy culminated in the mutiny at Invergordon. [7] The recurrence of strikes, however, meant that mining villages never had a chance to recover any kind of economic equilibrium. Women had no choice but to cope with the situation an a day to day basis.

Maria Stewart was very much aware of the unequal position of women in both community and Party and in 1930 complained about women being excluded from resolutions on employment and issues such as low wages, high rents and evictions.

The latter were commonplace and strategies were developed which did not prevent evictions taking place but made the job of the sheriff's officers very difficult. Furniture was lifted and put back into the house as quickly as it was dumped in the street. Maria became a District Councillor in 1935, was County Councillor for North Wemyss from 1945 - 1952, and fought against injustice in the system till the end of her life. [8]

Maria Stewart on left

Her whole family were involved in her political activities, her two youngest children were members of the Young Communist league and the youngest was one of Mary Docherty's 'Young Pioneers', a junior section of the Party. Mary was probably the most active worker between the wars, and unlike most of the other strong women of the era she was unmarried, and consequently had more freedom to take part in political activity. Some men objected to female participation and one described Mary as 'a wee yelp'. Few married women worked and those who did aroused resentment against 'two - income families' in the midst of high unemployment.

Until the 1920s, women's roles had been seen only as that of wives and mothers, and their political and economic activity was overlooked. In strikes, they were invaluable, providing the food and organisation required ; they sold pit papers with titles like The Spark, The Flame and The Lamp and played their part on picket lines, heckling and abusing blacklegs and burning effigies. They were involved in eviction protests and demonstrations at polling booths. In 1926 miners' wives were included in a two hundred strong contingent who left Thornton Station to attend a huge anti - strike demonstration in Edinburgh. In the thirties, Mary Docherty was in charge of the women's section of the Party and was widely involved with aid for Spain. She wasn't just interested in the miners' struggle for wages and conditions, she wanted to improve women's position in society . Mary's first public appearance as a speaker was in Lochgelly Town Hall at a meeting to celebrate International Women's Day; one of her last appearances, not long before her death in 1999, was at another such event. She published her autobiography, 'A Miner's Lass' at the age of eighty four, and her second book on her hero, Bob Selkirk four years later. [9]

Mary Docherty at home with her heroes

Mary had excellent credentials for a working class historian. Her grandmother had worked in the Fordell mines, in an old ladder pit, carrying creels of coal on her back from the coal face to the surface. At that time, miners still wore a metal collar with the name of the pit owner stamped on it. Mary's mother worked at the pit head and her father was a miner till he was blacklisted in 1921 for attempting to improve working practices. A committed Communist - she celebrated seventy years membership in 1996 - Mary suffered suspicion and prejudice for much of her life because of her political beliefs. At Secondary School in 1919 a teacher asked miners' daughters to identify themselves and lectured them on the harm their fathers were doing to the country. She recalled how in 1921, the military were brought in to break the strike which was caused by the miners refusal to return to pre-war rates of pay. [10]

The Dunfermline Press reported that in April that year 'Cowdenbeath ratepayers woke to find their burgh had been turned into an armed camp. Motor buses packed with soldiers and marines poured into Cowdenbeath and Lochgelly.' Military guards and wire barricades were placed round pit heads and soldiers from The Argyll and Sutherland Highlanders and The Seaforth Highlanders helped managers and officials to attend the furnaces. Children had to be fed at school. The miners resented the military being used to keep the pits going and after a clash with police, some retaliated by breaking shop windows in Cowdenbeath High Street. [11]

When Mary's father was blacklisted and unable to find work in any pit in the country, she rose at four thirty in the morning to help him deliver rolls, before starting her own day's work. Under her leadership, the Young Pioneers, the children's section of the Communist Party, played a big part in organising school strikes. Their demands included a May day holiday, the teaching of working class history in schools, the abolition of the strap and free meals and clothing for necessitous children. During the 1926 General Strike, she helped to organise a march to Dunfermline to demand that women and children be taken into the Poor House. According to the Poor Law, if the Poor house could not accommodate those asking for assistance, they had to be granted outdoor relief, that is, enough money to survive. With hundreds asking to be taken in, it was clearly an impossible situation so some financial help had to be given, as Mary well knew. In June 1926, five thousand people , miners and their supporters, turned up on the doorstep of Thornton Poorhouse and forced the hand of the local authority. [12]

Similar tactics were used elsewhere. Sarah Moore, from Addiewell in Lanarkshire, and an early pioneer of the labour movement, led a protest outside the parish office at West Calder against the decision to cease welfare payments to miners' dependants. Duncan Hay, the chief clerk at West Calder, took it upon himself to make the decision to stop payment. On a Friday morning Mrs Moore used bell ringers to summon claimants from the surrounding villages and marched them to West Calder. Hay refused to change his decision so the protesters camped out in front of the office and arrangements were made for food to be brought in. The protesters sat through Saturday and Sunday and so many turned up on Monday that Hay sent for the police 'to quell a riotous mob.' What they found was a group of mothers and toddlers good naturedly passing the time. Police tried to form them into an orderly queue but pushed so hard that one protester fell and cut his head on the pavement. The crowd got angry, police used batons, men overturned vehicles belonging to the Council and the police had to defend themselves. Mrs Moore, who had not been present, was sent for to restore order 'in the interest of public safety.' Hay rescinded his decision and protesters were instructed to attend the following morning to be paid. Mrs Moore went on to become a Lanark County Councillor and, during her eighteen years service till her death in 1947, the Convenor of the Public Health Committee. [13]

Sarah Moore with her 'rioters'

Abe Moffatt, in his autobiography, recalled that in 1930 during a strike at Shotts Coalfield, miners dependants were refused help. The Department of Health maintained that there was no money available, but hundreds of demonstrators gathered outside the Council Offices. He advised them to go inside and wait for the Health Board to come and put them out. The Board eventually agreed to pay them and the principle was ensured that dependants of miners would get parish relief when men were on strike. Moffatt also tells how, in 1933, soon after the eviction from his home of an unemployed miner, he was invited to the opening of the pit head baths at Lumphinnans No XI Colliery by Charles Carlow Reid. Leading coalmen and right wing leaders had been invited but a demonstration of about two to three hundred miners wives turned up too. Refused entry, they scattered and made their way into the meeting, chanting 'what about a key for the evicted miner?' They kept up their demonstration till Reid agreed to consider the case and the women demonstrators finished up sitting in the marquee with colliery staff and some of the policemen acting as waiters. [14]

This was an unusual outcome to a demonstration. Sometimes women were treated even more harshly than their male counterparts. In July 1924, Isabella O'Neill, a nineteen year old pit head worker, was charged with stealing coal. Her weekly wage was fourteen shillings and sixpence, of which twelve shillings and sixpence was deducted for rent. She was the family's sole breadwinner. During the 1926 strike, two miners wives from Blantyre were arrested and charged with 'besetting', a law which had long fallen into disuse but was revived during miners strikes. Besetting originally meant 'surrounding with hostile intentions' or 'to occupy so as to allow no-one to go out or in' and so could be used against picketers or someone just standing outside the home of a striking miner.

Jennie Lee was born in Lochgelly in 1904 and in her autobiography she wrote that it was the General Strike of 1926 that shaped her life more than any other experience. She described how every day, a procession led by pipe bands made its way to the pit. There were fights with police, house windows broken and fires lit at the pit. Police used batons against the people of Glencraig, including at least one woman, and surrounded the houses of demonstrators who were hauled out of bed and arrested.

Jennie's father, a pit deputy, was deeply involved in Labour politics; her grandfather

with Keir Hardie, had fought to build up a labour Trade Union and Co-operative movement and was disputes secretary for the Fife and Clackmannan Miners Union. The years 1926 to 1929, in the aftermath of the strike, saw a repetition of the struggle of those early years. Men were blacklisted for trade union activities, children went hungry and badly clothed and women died because of lack of nourishment and medical care. Jennie was elected as MP for North Lanark in 1929 and took her seat as the youngest member in the Commons.

Jennie Lee on a visit to Fife in 1983

In her twenty seven years in Parliament, Jennie was on the National Executive of the Labour Party, Parliamentary Secretary of State at the Ministry of Public Buildings and Works, Under Secretary of State for Education and Science, Minister of State and Chairman of the Labour Party. Her achievements included the setting up of The Open University but she did not forget her early years as a teacher in Glencraig where the coal bings reached almost into the playground and the authorities maintained that this posed no danger to public health. [15]

Jennie Lee wrote about police using batons and seventeen men being arrested but Anni Cairns of Kennoway was more personally involved. In 1984, in the middle of being a self-styled 'hells-fired fund-raiser' of our Striking Miners and Women's Action Group, she took time to write an account of that night in 1926, when the lockout was in full swing. A babe in arms at the time, Anni grew up with the story. Miners from Glencraig and Lochgelly joined to do battle with the riot squads but the Lochgelly miners scattered , leaving the Glencraig men outnumbered. They fought ferociously, defending themselves with pick-axe handles as weapons before escaping. Lorry loads of blacklegs rolled into Glencraig between one and two in the morning and the rounding up began of the marked men, the hard core of resistance against the bosses' demands.

'Twas shortly after two of that ghastly night when the so called police came to our house, eight blue clad Johnnie laws to uplift my father who was a small boned fine skinned man, just five foot three when standing tall, non -political till the exploitation of an hour a day more for a bob a day less made him see red'.

Casimerixz Marcinkewixz had left his hometown of Siwalki in Lithuania and with his parents and two younger brothers, and his wife and her parents, had come to settle in Fife. He was entered on the Aliens Register as Russian-Lithuanian and in Fife was given the name Charlie Mitchell and usually called 'Wee Chairlie'.

He was waiting fully dressed for the policemen, but they dragged him out and before throwing him into a police van, laid into him with their truncheons. A widow who lived opposite opened her door , hoping to intervene but her skull was smashed by a truncheon which threw her back indoors. The same treatment was meted out to others. Two escaped. One, Miles Dolan , had been sent away by his mother into hiding in Cowdenbeath but the police forced their way into her house and wrecked it in an attempt to learn his whereabouts. To save her further harassment, the two escapees offered to give themselves up on the assurance that they wouldn't be manhandled or beaten. All the men were tried under the Riot Act and Miles had been beaten so severely that it was not till he stood up to answer his name that his mother recognised him. All save one of the men were convicted and sentenced to terms of imprisonment. Miles got hard labour in Barlinnie Jail.

Wee Chairlie had been left to the last. The court intended to make an example of him because he was the only one who wasn't a British subject. He was a Bolshie from Lithuania. Thus he was tried and sentenced to deportation, and his wife, two younger brothers and both sets of parents were included in the order. After being sentenced, he asked to be allowed to speak and, being granted this, he played his trump card. 'It's only my bairns I'm asking to be considered,' he said, 'they're British born subjects. Are they to be deported too?'

His question threw the prosecutors into confusion for in their haste, they hadn't spared a moment's consideration for the children. 'Twas within their legal right.' wrote Anni, 'to deport the gawdamned foreigners but a different proposition to impose such a sentence on wee Britishers, and therefore, they had no alternative than to quash the deportation and conduct a retrial.' When Charlie was eventually released from prison, he could not sit down for three months because of the daily kicking he received. [16]

Anni remembered how she was a nosy lassie and instead of going out to play she would sit and listen to the political chinwagging . With such a family history, which would have been repeated in varying degrees throughout the coal fields of Scotland, it is surprising that more women did not come to public attention. One who did was Helen Crauford ,but her background was totally unlike Anni's.

Born the daughter of a master baker in the Gorbals district of Glasgow in 1877, Helen came from a comfortable middle class background. She was made aware of women's inferiority at a very young age, when her brothers were given a shilling to spend at a fair and she got only sixpence. She grew up in Ipswich but returned to Glasgow in her teens, was shocked by the misery and poverty of Glasgow workers, and appalled by the broken down bodies, bowlegs and rickets that were prevalent. She married the minister of a church in Anderston, a parish holding some of Glasgow's worst slums. Her awareness of the condition of Glasgow workers was to develop into a passionate desire to change these conditions and a tireless struggle to achieve this end. She began to listen to Socialist propaganda at outdoor meetings and, with her two step daughters, soon became involved with the suffrage movement, feeling that if mothers had some say, then things would change. She had faith in women's ability to change their condition if they could be wakened, organised and allowed to take part in making laws for their country. She made several visits to Fife and wrote that miners never took rent for halls used for suffragist meetings and collections were always good.

Her involvement with the militant suffragette movement began when she heard Helen Fraser speaking at a meeting in Rothesay ,and she was later sent to prison several times for her activities, including a month in Holloway in 1912 for breaking windows at the home of the Minister of Education in London. Other terms of imprisonment were spent in Perth and in Glasgow where she again broke windows, this time at an army recruiting office, and was released under The Cat and Mouse Act after an eight day hunger strike. This Act allowed women to be freed from jail when their lives were in danger from fasting and enabled them to be re-arrested at any time without having committed further offences. Each time Helen was arrested, she immediately went on hunger strike again.

During the First War, she became Secretary of The Women's Peace Crusade and was twice arrested for anti-war work, appearing in the dock with Willie Gallagher and other Socialist leaders. She joined the Independent Labour Party and became its Vice-President, travelling throughout Britain to address meetings. She visited Russia in 1920 and met Lenin and on her return became Secretary of The Workers International Relief Organisation. This came into being in response to the disastrous famine in the Volga provinces of Russia. The rich grain growing areas of Russia had been destroyed by seven years of global and civil war and in 1921,a prolonged drought brought famine and starvation to tens of thousands of people. Ordinary people , including mining families, contributed to the famine fund . People have expressed wonder that Russian miners gave financial help during miners' strikes, but the Russians saw it as a debt of honour, a repayment of the help given in the famine. In the aftermath of the first war, Helen also was responsible through the W.I.R for bringing relief to starving children in Germany in the famine years of the nineteen twenties.

In 1926, the General Strike lasted for only nine days, but the miners continued for a further nine months before they were starved into submission. Helen travelled the country, raising support in terms of money, food and encouragement for the locked out men and their families and paid many visits to Fife. The W.I.R concentrated on helping the children and Helen went with a lorry full of parcels into the pit villages and passed on messages of support. In 1921, she joined the newly formed Communist Party in Britain and remained faithful till the end. In the thirties, she was appointed secretary of the Anti-Fascist Organisation in Glasgow and helped to ensure that Oswald Mosely was never allowed to hold a meeting there. In 1945, at the age of sixty eight, she was elected to the Town Council in Dunoon, where she spent her later years and kept up a voluminous correspondence in the press on local and international affairs .

Of her visits to mining areas, she wrote that she met intelligent men and women. scientists, musicians, artists, astronomers and geologists. In 1926, she spoke at meetings all over Fife and recruited twenty three new party members in two days and in all achieved a total of one hundred and forty two new female members.

Helen was, on the surface, an unlikely candidate for Communism. Coming from a Conservative background and married to a minister, she could have had a comfortable life. Long before her husband died in 1914, she was involved in working class radicalism and even people who disagreed with her political stance admired her as a truly remarkable woman who commanded universal respect. [17]

Helen Crawfurd (left) on one of her many visits to Methil 1926 General strike

Distributing food parcels at Lochore

The Woman Worker

NO. 2   MAY, 1926   ONE PENNY

HOW FIFE WAS FED IN LOCKOUT OF 1921

Dear Comrade,

We in Methil commenced communal feeding first in the Fife coalfield, due to the fact that we had experienced short time from the datum line strike of November, 1920. Commenced first week of lock-out with two meals per day. We divided Methil into five districts (population, 7,000); and put women in charge of cooking arrangements at each centre. Men detailed to do all dirty and heavy work—splitting firewood, cleaning cooking utensils, carrying coal, etc.

One woman was responsible at each kitchen or centre for amount of food, etc., required.

A central committee for the five centres was composed of local Union Branch Committee, with two representatives from each centre, who met every day.

A meeting of all employed at each centre was held every Fr

TYPICAL MINERS' HOMES

Message from A. J. Cook to Miners' Wives & Womenfolk

BE LOYAL

SOME CONTRASTS

By

ELIZABETH GLADING.

Sir Alan Burgoyne, M.P., in the House of Commons, with the usual bad taste of a supporter of the present Government, referred to the Soviet State as " a noisome hulk, rotten from truck to keelson," embellishing his speech with similar flights of fancy. Yet in this " rotten " State they are prepared to discuss the principle of removing taxation from the poorer peasants and taxing only the well-to-do. On the other hand, in this well-equipped "Ship of State," which is under the direction of Sir Alan Burgoyne, Jix, and Company and other such choice spirits, a millionaire shipowner, who made over six millions out of the blood and sweat of the last war, escaped taxation by making Jersey his place of

The following stirring message has been sent to the "Worker", by A. J. Cook, and we hope that our readers will do their best to bring it to the notice of all miners' wives and womenfolk:—

Industrially and politically the wives of the workers of this country have been kept in ignorance of the economic facts appertaining to industry.

They have been made use of politically by every party without determining the policy which they were supporting.

They have suffered in every industrial lock-out or strike without having a say of any kind.

I therefore welcome the issue of a woman's paper that gives clearly the working class point of view, especially during the present crisis.

Miners' wives in particular now know how the capitalist class, with their various organisations, are prepared to use them against their husbands and sons, as was evidenced by the recent demonstration in London.

It behoves the women to play their part to defend their homes, and to protect their children in the great class struggle which will mean constant slavery and serfdom for them and their children, or the emancipation of the whole working class by the overthrow of capitalism and the establishment of the co-operative commonwealth.

Actions speak louder than words. Duty calls every woman at this moment to take her stand with the men in the movement to defend their rights and drive back the oppressors.

cooking quality, and alteration of food supplied was discussed. Also complaints from either staffs at kitchens or those being served with food.

The women did not attend many meetings, but we (the local Union Branch Committee) visited each centre every day and received suggestions, complaints, etc., from them at the kitchens. The result was that we were able to keep in touch with every point re feeding.

In addition to our kitchens we managed to get the Education Authority to put into operation "Clause 2, Section 6 of the Education (Scotland) Act, 1908 (as modified by the Fifth Schedule to the Education (Scotland) Act, 1918)" thereby getting all school children supplied with three meals per day.

Later on, due to numbers of non-school children being supplied, we managed to get the Council to agree to supply us with the meal which we in some cases distributed, and in others (where the parents were "loose" or the mother sick, or having a large family of youngsters) we cooked at the kitchens.

In addition we supplied the children with bread, butter, kippers, sausages, etc., for which we were paid weekly by the Council at the rate of 6d. per day for every non-school child.

After three weeks of lock-out we were in Methil supplying three meals per day, which was continued until three weeks after lock-out, after which two were supplied for a short time.

has escaped taxation by similar means

Under the heading "My Lady Takes to Trousers," the Press a few days ago reported the latest fad amongst the idle rich. It must thrill the heart of Mrs.

Write to us about it

Smith, of Poplar, to read that dressy pyjamas, gorgeously embroidered in Eastern fashion, and trimmed with priceless lace, are the correct wear for smoking parties. It is true, perhaps, that the only smoking she ever does is when she fires the chimney to avoid the cost of a sweep. It certainly suggests a further use for father's old pants. Tommy Smith has usually been the un-

Conditions are now greatly altered; non-mining districts being in almost as bad a plight as we are, and the result will mean concentrating on the Parish Councils, in addition to the Child Welfare and Education Authority.

Parish scale in this parish (Wemyss) is £1 for man and wife, 7/6 for first child and 4/- for each subsequent child. We have already suggested to the women that they should apply themselves.

The Woman Worker

Issued by the Women's Department Communist Party of Great Britain.

———o———

All communications should be addressed to THE WOMAN WORKER
16, King Street, London, W. C. 2

MAY DAY, 1926

Never was a more fateful May Day in the history of the workers. The whole country waits tense, expectant, wondering what this May Day will bring forth. The mineowners in flinging down the gauntlet to the miners have challenged the right of the whole of the working class to existence on the most meagre scale.

If that challenge is not withdrawn, then May Day means—conflict!

In this conflict women must play their part. Too long have we stood aside wringing our hands in helpless impotence. Too long have we shut ourselves up inside our little houses to brood over our wrongs.

Now is the time for action! The employers are banking on the weakness of the women, and are endeavouring to turn them against their men-folk in strikes or lock-outs.

Remember if the struggle comes it has been caused by the employing class, whose object is to bring down the standard of living of all the workers.

Women know that it is impossible to feed and clothe their families properly on the present wages.

The men, if they fight, will be fighting for bread. Women must help.

By taking part in the May Day demonstrations, by offering their services to the Councils of Action, by building up really effective organisation of women.

Women's Councils of Action

There is a weapon lying close at hand. In Manchester, Sheffield, and Mansfield, women's organisations have sent delegates to conferences, and out of these conferences have built up joint committees consisting of delegates from working women's organisations.

The letter we print from Fife gives some indication of what can be done to feed the workers when trouble is on.

It will be easily seen how women can help in this.

If a Council of Action exists in a locality the Women's Council should be part of it and act with it.

Then they could organise street meetings to explain the issues to the women, use their influence in the Co-operatives through the Guilds and at the General Meetings, to induce them to grant credits.

Each woman delegate who is a member of the Council should realise her responsibility and do her best to see that the organisation she represents supports with its whole strength all that the Council undertakes.

Speakers can be sent from the Council to all the women's organisations to appeal for help. Picketing, message carrying, protecting food stuffs, visiting farmers and shopkeepers, organising food kitchens and creches, where older women can release active young mothers for more strenuous work.

Out of this we will then be able to form women's auxiliary units of our Workers' Defence Corps.

So to our tasks. There is a job for every woman, old or young, and if this job is done the victory of the workers is assured.

CHAPTER ELEVEN

THE BEST SUMMER?

Because of the 1840 Commission of Inquiry into Children's Employment, we have first hand accounts of living and working conditions of ordinary nineteenth century mining women in Scotland. Very few contemporary twentieth century accounts are in existence because it was only recently realised that this aspect of history was worthy of research. In the 1980s, research into women's memories of their work place was carried out in Stirling. Eighty women, who worked in various industries in the early years of the twentieth century, were interviewed and recorded. Transcripts of the tapes, held in The Smith Museum and Art Gallery Archives, contain several references to life among the pits in the Stirling area. Though conditions had vastly improved since 1842, by today's standards life in the twenties sounded horrendous. There is no sign of self-pity, however, indeed the impression is of a hard but satisfying existence. How much the passage of years is responsible one can only guess.

'We used to get up at six to gather coal, up to the top of the bing, fill our bags with wee bits of coal and sticks and everything, and hurl it back to the coal house in a wheelbarrow. But when the pit started and the waggons went up we had to stop. A niece of mine got her fingers run over with a waggon coming up. She was too slow taking her hand out. It's what we had to do. Coal was only one and three a bag but we couldn't afford it.' [1]

'We had three miles to walk to school, we got up at six. My father and three brothers were on nightshift all their lives. They'd come home about half past six and my mother would have a big pot of porridge on the hob. Then they got ham and eggs and slept till twelve and then played billiards or whatever was on in the village.'

Though the men had their clubs and pubs, women had fewer organised leisure activities. Nevertheless they had a vibrant social life, revolving round the home and back greens.

'In the clear nights the women would come out and play rounders or skipping....'

'We'd meet at the corner of one of the rows and one man would bring out his melodeon and we'd dance till ten. We had to be in and the door locked when my father went out on nightshift.' [2]

Though the roles of men and women were sharply divided, sometimes they overlapped: 'My father was secretary of the Manor Powys branch of the miners insurance from 1912-1945. Mother took it over for four years when he was away at the war.' [3]

Strikes figured largely in memories. About 1926, one said that 'My husband was on strike for seven months and we had to go back home or we'd have been in debt. You had to get stuff on credit. We got four shillings once from Russian miners. Pits were not as safe then as they are now and it was nothing new for your man to get an accident. You just got on with it and used your initiative.' [4]

Women waiting for news.
Lindsay Disaster Kelty 1957

Accidents were commonplace. Before the first war, an average of eleven hundred miners were killed each year and five hundred injured every day. Until the 1920s boys as young as fourteen were killed underground. Pit disasters made headlines and funds were raised by public subscription but the widows whose men died alone had to depend on the charity of their neighbours and the goodwill of the coal owner, who could demand that she vacate the house immediately if there was no son to take the father's place. By the turn of the century most miners were members of Friendly Societies, but funerals might cost the equivalent of two weeks' wages and if too many claims had to be made, as in Mauricewood, at Penicuik in 1889, when sixty men were killed, only a few shillings could be paid to each. After the Donibristle and Hill of Beath disasters in 1901 when thirteen men were killed, The Fife and Kinross Miners Accident (Permanent) Fund was set up to relieve distress for widows and children of without sufficient means of support. Thirteen widows with forty children were given assistance. There was no Health Service and no sickness benefit.

'We got no money when he was off sick. When my husband was invalided out of the pit, I started work at fifty and worked till I was sixty three.' [5]

'You didn't have money for new clothes. You took them off at night and washed them ready for the next morning.' In spite of hardship, humour is very much in evidence. '1926 was the best summer miners ever had, it was the only time they ever got sunburned and we didn't need coal fires. The ladies cleaned out the wash boilers, the men gathered potatoes and vegetables from the farmers and it was all cooked in the boiler. You got a can of soup and a half loaf.' [6]

The pits provided the livelihood for whole villages so everyone was hard hit. A strike meant the loss, not of one wage, but of several. For some families, soup kitchens were the only source of food. Others depended on help from daughters in service or in other strike free employment. Sometimes three or four sisters worked together at the pit head and in some homes, the entire family with the exception of the mother, were employed in some capacity in mining.

By 1931, unemployment in coalfields was up to forty one per cent and those still in work were paid on average half the wages in other industries. Medical studies in mining areas showed that over one million people were suffering from malnutrition and a special Miners National Distress Fund was set up. Women were sometimes able to find work in the fields, turnip thinning or 'tattie howkin' for two and six a day but any income had to be reported and many were taken to court and fined for earning while claiming public assistance. Until Parish Councils were abolished in 1930 they were responsible for providing financial assistance which was an early form of social security organised on a local level and each council could draw up its own scales of payment. In some places, help consisted of food vouchers, issued weekly according to the number of children in the family. The depression years of the early thirties, with mass unemployment placed an intolerable burden on local authorities and the first steps were taken the first steps were taken to transfer responsibility to the national exchequer. It was not till 1948 after the foundation of the Welfare State that the problems of dealing with deserted and separated wives and unmarried mothers moved from the local to national level.

People could still enjoy themselves, however. While much of the country remained agricultural, there were fairs and markets, annual games and horse shows, with dancing and 'Punch's Opera' and merry-go-rounds. Villages organised annual balls, 'penny readings' which usually cost sixpence, concert parties and theatricals. Will Fyffe the character actor and comedian, visited Cowdenbeath with his father's portable theatre. Brass and pipe bands flourished as did musical and operatic societies. By 1900 Lochgelly had two literary societies and and a scientific society and library; lectures were given on education, mechanics, geology, theology, history and science. A trawl through newspapers from the nineteen hundreds reveals a vast array of societies, from antiquarian to zoology by way of cage birds, horticulture, literature, music and drama.

By the 1960s there were over sixty dramatic clubs in Scottish mining communities with Fife leading the way. The Bowhill Players, led by miner playwright and poet Joe Corrie were famous. Bowhill also had a world renowned Burns Club whose guests included Norman McCaig and Hugh Mc Diarmid. The outstanding social event of the year was the Miners' Gala, which in Fife began as a celebration of the eight hour day . As well as local village galas, there were county wide gatherings with Highland Games and pipe and brass bands from all collieries taking part, and attended by speakers like Emmanuel Shinwell. National galas were held annually in Holyrood Park in Edinburgh. Christmas Day was not a holiday but Hogmanay was, though the two days off were unpaid.

Every sport under the sun was catered for. All mining villages had their own football teams, some had several and even an occasional women's one. Cricket was not so

Cowdenbeath Ladies Football Team. During they 1921 strike they raised funds for soup kitchens by playing against the policemen who had been brought in to keep order. A Lochore ladies team played against men dressed in women's clothing

popular and young children, with hardly a stitch to their backs, marvelled at these people who could afford to buy special clothes to play a game.

Although coal owners took the credit for introducing amenities like football pitches and bowling greens, most of the money came from the miners' pay packets and without their enthusiasm, nothing could have been achieved. Mining families even had to pay for the pit baths. The Coal Mines Bill of 1911 was passed to provide bathing facilities; but with so many loopholes that it was possible for owners to duck responsibility; and until long after nationalisation, miners had to pay the full costs of washing pit dirt from their bodies.

Bowling was one activity that women were encouraged to take part in, and for them there was also the church, the co-operative guilds and the Women's Rural Institute, begun in Canada in 1895 and introduced to Britain in 1915. As well as life's enjoyments, women shared its tragedies. Holman in his History of Cowdenbeath wrote that 'in times of rejoicing - birth marriage or christening, a next door neighbour is of great assistance and enters the spirit of the event as much as the woman herself. In time of mourning and sadness she also mourns, In cases of sickness, death or accident, the latter in a mining community, coming upon them at a moment's notice, a sympathetic neighbour is a friend indeed and it is to her the afflicted one goes for sympathy in the full knowledge that she will not be denied.'

It is probably this awareness of living continually on the edge of a precipice that engendered the closeness of mining communities. Their separation from the rest of society and dependence on their own efforts to achieve any improvements gave purpose and cohesion to their social life.

At the beginning of World War II, many miners volunteered for active service but mining was a reserved occupation and those who did manage to slip through the net were quickly returned to their collieries. The Essential Work Order imposed in 1941 brought a return of eighteenth century law - a miner could not leave his employment, but could not be dismissed either. His reward, however, did not recognise his status as an essential worker. In 1944, at number eighty one down on the national wages scale, miners went on strike to force the government to agree to a national minimum wage, but were denounced as traitors who were destroying the economic basis of the state.

Living conditions during the war had worsened in many areas because water had to be pumped on to bings to suppress the glow from fires caused by spontaneous combustion and this, with the smoke from coal fires, meant that much of the countryside was enveloped in a sooty cloud. Women had to cope with shortages and ration books but food rationing led to changes in domestic practice. The introduction of canteens meant that the tradition of the piece box was not as essential as it had been. Meals and snacks were available at the pit head and by 1946 there were twenty five canteens in the Fife and Clackmannan coal fields, catering for over fifteen thousand men. Changes to women's working conditions came too, with the introduction of pit head baths. When the first pit head baths were opened in 1926, no consideration was given to the provision of facilities for women but by 1945, four pits in Fife - Bowhill, Minto, Michael and Wellesley – employing between them two hundred and twenty female pit head workers, has women's baths.

For mining families, as for all working-class families, the introduction of Family Allowances in 1945 went a small way to lighten the economic burden. Two years later, however, the coal owners were attempting to re-introduce Sunday funerals to avoid shifts being cancelled.

The employment of women at the pit head remained a bone of contention but on a much smaller scale. During the war, there had been a sharp increase in the numbers employed, though it was not till 1943 that uniformity of wages was introduced and this was never more than two thirds of men's wages. Numbers dwindled post war and in 1954 Margaret Herbison suggested that no new female recruits should be accepted in the industry. The Coal Board and the NUM agreed that when women retired or left they would not be replaced and where possible, existing workers were given jobs as canteen assistants or switchboard operators. The last female pit head workers, however, remained till 1967 leaving only when the Minto pit in Fife closed .

By that time, it was not just the women's jobs that were on the line. The belief that Britain's energy needs could be met by cheap oil from the Middle East and from the new nuclear power industry meant that a systematic programme of pit closures was put into operation and miners wives and families became 'industrial gypsies' as they were forced to move from place to place in search of jobs. Mining villages were basically extended families but the new deal meant that women were uprooted from their own close knit communities and resettled in English coalfields where, though the work was similar, the language and traditions were alien.

In six years Scotland lost thirty nine per cent of its pits. Though small local strikes took place in the fifties and sixties, there had been no national action since 1926. It was believed that no such action could ever happen again but the entire British coalfield was out on strike for seven weeks from January 1972, the reason for discontent, as always, poor rates of pay A Commission of Inquiry awarded substantial pay rises and this success gave a new sense of unity and purpose, and an unfounded belief in their ability to withstand government pressure.

The history of miners' strikes in the seventies and eighties has been well documented elsewhere but the struggle revealed a new dimension in British political life. The 1984 strike was not about wages and conditions but a last ditch and ultimately unsuccessful attempt to save the mining industry from total annihilation. It also demonstrated, for the first time, the power of women to be in the forefront of industrial disputes. In mining communities, women's groups were set up which didn't just organise soup kitchens but took their place in the in the political arena as well as on picket lines in defence of jobs. Unarmed, underfed and sometimes carrying babies or toddlers, they faced police equipped with horses, dogs, truncheons and riot gear.

FAMINE CONDITIONS IN THE BRITISH MINEFIELDS

MEN, WOMEN AND CHILDREN STARVING

Since their defeat in 1926 the economic position of the miners has steadily grown worse. They have been compelled to relinquish every right and concession won during the past century of struggle. Almost 900 000 are receiving 30% less real wages than in 1913. Over 300 000 are workless and of these 200 000 will never again be employed in the industry.

All over the entire coalfield there is terrible poverty. Large districts previously employing thousands are now silent and derelict. The various town treasuries are bankrupt. Municipal services are at a standstill. Property values have touched bottom. Taxation is unbearably high. New industries are impossible.

Hunger diseases are rampant. Infantile mortality is so much on the increase that the Minister of Health has been compelled to open an official enquiry. Thousands of

school children are undernourished, sick, and subnormal. Men, Women, and children are in rags and unable to face with safety the approaching winter. Thousands of homes are without bedclothes, heat or food and are absolutely dependant on outside assistance.

Every day additional hundreds are refused state

Showing typical Pit head machinery

INTERNATIONAL RELIEF ACTION IMMEDIATELY REQUIRED

assistance from the Labour Exchanges. On the plea of enforced Government economy the Boards of Guardians are reducing the amount of help given to distressed Miners families. In some areas hundreds of families are forced to live on less than 7d per head per day for food. Young men living with their parents receive no assistance from any source whatever.

The position of the expectant miner's wife is dangerously cruel. Births daily take place without adequate preparations or necessary bedclothes. Poor neighbours on occasions have collected amongst themselves enough rags to keep the new baby warm. Milk allowances at most of the Welfare Centres have also been reduced.

Last February the Workers International Relief investigated conditions in the minefields. It

later organised the Miners Relief Committee (W.I.R.) which during the past few months has collected hundreds of pounds and distributed over 12 tons of clothing and boots amongst the starving miners and their dependants.

Two years after the 1926 strike the effects were still being felt

CHAPTER TWELVE

1984 – A VERY HARD YEAR

1984. The year of Big Brother, the year when laws that had lain dormant for centuries were brought out, dusted off and used against the mining communities of Britain. A year in which one hundred thousand miners lost a year's earnings and were submerged in debts that would haunt them for years; when almost nine thousand miners would be arrested; when men who stood up for the right to earn their living as their forebears had done for generations, were reviled, demonised and criminalised; when the relationship between the people and the forces of law and order were well-nigh destroyed; which left communities torn and divided; and which brought to an end the mining industry in this country. The year of a strike at the end of which Margaret Thatcher would smugly echo the words of Stanley Baldwin in 1926, 'It took us time to get it right.'

1984 was also the year that provided a defining moment in the lives of many miners' wives. For a whole year, they worked, kept their homes and families together and raised enough money to keep the strike going longer than was thought possible. They'd been cold, underfed, unable to afford the basic necessities of life; taken their place on public platforms, on picket lines; were manhandled by police and locked up in cells. They'd forged links with women's groups fighting for other causes; had achieved a solidarity never before experienced and an understanding of what women in other countries felt about their place in society. For a whole year their lives, relationships and financial situation were turned upside down. Their involvement in the strike brought them an awareness of what could be done - as individuals and as part of a bigger group. Their sphere of influence widened out from their homes and villages to the whole world. From trying to prevent the government from destroying the local economy they reached out to grasp the ramifications of the anti-apartheid movement in South Africa and women's rights in Chile and Nicaragua. Then they were expected to drop everything and pick up their lives where they'd been put down a year before as if nothing had happened in between. As Cath Cunningham explained, they had 'to adjust to normality, whatever normality is', but all that remained was a vacuum. [1]

Jean Stead, a journalist closely involved with mining communities during the strike called her book *'Never the Same Again'*. The history of the strike has been well documented but Stead's book is one of a handful which deals with the women's role. The Lothian Women's Support Group produced an excellent collection of anecdotes by women and children in Lothian mining villages who, as the title says, were *'Living The Strike.* Cath Cunningham and Marge Givens from Fife, along with an unnamed representative of the Dalkeith Women's Support Group are featured in *Grit and Diamonds, Women in Scotland Making History, 1980-1990.* The title comes from a member of the Dalkeith Women's Support Group, who felt they had achieved victory, of a kind by people's acceptance of their role in what had always been a male dominated struggle. Till 1984 women's function had been seen as providing meals and washing dishes; that year they were not following their men but were fighting shoulder to shoulder with them. 'We learned patience and determination. We have got the grit and it's the grit that eventually that polishes the diamonds.' [2] Yet these were the same people that Coal Board chairman Sir Ian McGregor described as 'the enemies within.'

A group of miners wives in Mauchline in Ayrshire produced a small booklet, *A Very Hard Year,* with their account of the year long battle. Mauchline was one of twenty four strike centres serving Ayrshire's last two pits. Like other mining communities the village was no stranger to pit closures. Since 1961, forty seven mines and almost eleven thousand jobs had gone. Mauchline's own pit had closed in 1968 and by 1984 only one hundred and eighteen mining families remained. This contributed to their sense of isolation and the feeling that they were outside the normal support systems which operated in villages where the bulk of families relied on mining. Though women from the local strikers support groups attended rallies elsewhere, few outsiders visited.

Jean Stead's links with mining communities in Scotland were in Polmaise, near Stirling and Bilston Glen and Monktonhall in Lothian. In January 1984, miners at Polmaise Colliery were told that their pit would close despite the government having already spent fifteen million pounds of a twenty four million pound investment to open up new seams which would have provided coal for another thirty years. Men gave up the chance of huge redundancy payments for the sake of keeping their jobs going. Over and over again in the months that followed the miners were asked why they were striking. 'We've nowhere else to go,' they said. If the pits closed there were no other jobs. The miners began the strike but couldn't have kept it going without the support of their women.

Women didn't want to see their men on the dole and their children rejected by employers. Miners were supposed to receive sixteen pounds a week as strike pay from the NUM, so that amount was kept off any welfare benefits but it was impossible for the Union to pay its members anything, because the government had sequestrated its funds. Young single miners got no DHSS money because they were also supposed to get this sixteen pounds, and mothers had to feed and clothe them without help from the state. [3]

After the strike began, Polmaise women started collecting their own funds and took over the Miners Welfare kitchen to provide meals for strikers and their families. They took collecting boxes on to the streets of Glasgow and were arrested for doing so, made speeches and organised fund raising campaigns. Women became adept at dealing with the authorities, learning about welfare rights and standing up for themselves and their neighbours. Many worked part time but got organised into women's committees, made up rotas for meals and organised creches, and at the same time began to make their presence felt on the picket lines.

Fallin village, near Polmaise Colliery, was organised on collective lines and families were given vouchers to buy meat. Money came from other workers, from Imperial Tobacco, from Grangemouth, where dock workers gave twenty five per cent of their wages each week ,and many others. Support came from abroad. At Christmas, 1984, thousands of turkeys were donated, and one hundred thousand toys, ranging from rattles to railways, balloons to bicycles arrived from French trade unionists. For children in Lothian mining villages too, that Christmas was a communal affair with gifts from France, visits to a pantomime in Edinburgh and a circus in Glasgow. It was a bright spot in an otherwise dark year. But Christmas wasn't bright for everyone. Police cars were everywhere and 'even to drive into the yard of the Miners Welfare made you feel as though you might be picked up and arrested.' [4]

In Fife, there were ten strike centres, the main one being The Dysart Strike Centre for Women. The Lothian Women's Committee co-ordinated twenty eight support groups set up by wives of miners from Bilston Glen and Monktonhall Collieries. To begin with, the emphasis was on running soup kitchens and making meals, but gradually women's activities broadened to fund raising and going on picket lines. As the scale of activities widened, so too did their confidence and women found themselves on public platforms, speaking to mass rallies all over the country. The courage to do it came from the strength of their feelings, the need to protect not just the mining industry but their homes, families and way of life. One of the first events that the Fife women were involved in was a demonstration in Edinburgh called by the Scottish Trades Union Congress with the theme of 'Victorian Values'. Women from outside the coal fields attended and provided moral support for those who were hesitant about taking part. Financial support also came from a wide range of countries and social classes. Without this starvation would have been a fact of life.

Moral support was as important as provision of food. Women always take the brunt of financial hardship, even in normal circumstances, tending to put their own needs last. 'At the kitchen we called ourselves the plastic shoe brigade . None of us could afford shoes during the strike until we came across these plastic sandals at the market for £1.99 a pair....They lasted till about October then you got a kind of frostbite on your toes.' [5] Things normally taken for granted, like washing powder, soap and talc became luxury items. Women's groups from other parts of the country provided necessities of life, basic things like sanitary towels, pants and tights, and all new babies were provided with a layette. It is this feeling of solidarity with other women that comes through in written accounts, the feeling that others out there understood what was important and did something about it. Clothes came from jumble sales and grants were given by the education department for school clothes. Children had to suffer the taunts of fellow pupils.

'What I didnae like was at school I couldnae pay for my cooking lessons. Other kids would make out we were on charity which made me mad.' [6]

'Some were against us getting free dinners. I kent no tae listen to them.' [7]

Cowdenbeath High Street

Fife miners wives on the picket lines at Cowdenbeath workshops. Earlier in the day they had marched to Seafield Colliery to demand the release of coal for the elderly and sick. The manager refused to see them

What made life bearable for most people was the knowledge that everyone was in the same boat and the general feeling was that there was no point in complaining, they just got on with their lives. It was a time of sharing, their last loaf of bread if need be, and one meal a day was normal. Television sets were repossessed and electricity supplies cut off. But it wasn't all gloom and doom. For the women there was the chance of adventure. Invitations were coming in to attend rallies and to speak on public platforms, buses going to Yorkshire or London . Sometimes they drew lots to decide who would go. Some of them had never been out of Scotland and meeting different people, seeing different places, and getting involved broadened their horizons, made them politically aware. In little mining villages, women had read the papers and watched the news but felt that it didn't really affect them. But that all changed .The women, whose only financial expertise was in budgeting the weekly income, learned to learn to cope with managing the sums of money that came in from all over the world.

Clothes and food came too, from Holland, France, East and West Germany. The government tried to block food from Russia but the dockers wouldn't let them. Russian scented tea and tinned mince were part of the staple diet for some time. Most foreigners were shocked at the pitiful amount of welfare benefits people in this country were entitled to. Support groups organised outings and holidays. An organisation called 'Women Against Pit Closures' (WAPC) had been formed just before the march and rally against pit closures which took place in London in August 1984 . From a small local meeting in Barnsley , the WAPC became a national organisation linking all women's support groups. A branch from Sheffield organised a trip to East Germany and also organised a petition to the Queen, asking her to intervene in the strike. An estimated crowd of twenty three thousand women, including a hundred or so from Lothian, and train and bus loads from all over Scotland, converged on London. Arthur Scargill's wife Ann, was one of the women chosen to hand in the petition but in the end it made no difference to the outcome, the rally demonstrated the amount of support in the country as a whole for the cause of mineworkers families.

Women joined the men on the picket lines and like them were picked on by the police. Some, like Jean Hamilton, were arrested and charged with assaulting the police. She was for foot eleven inches tall. "I'll never forget it,' she said,' A young policeman, G59, with a wee moustache, lifted me, one arm up my back and another arm round my neck. I could feel my throat getting pressed in tighter and tighter and my feet kicking away like mad. I was thrown against the van and sworn at.' [8]

The costs of policing the strike was phenomenal and people were sickened that the government could finance the picket lines but not the pits . Much of the bitterness of the strike was directed against the police who seemed to enjoy their job and the media who portrayed the miners as bully boys. In many cases it was the other way about. 'Police outnumbered men many times…...if a push came on someone was sure to lose their job. Why? For shouting scab……' . [9]

'Living under the truncheon reign, step out of line and feel the pain' [10] summed up a good deal about the strike as far as the Mauchline women were concerned. Miners re-actions to women on the picket lines were very mixed. Some disapproved totally, be-lieving that their place was in the kitchen, keeping the food supply going. Others supported women's presence in principle but were genuinely afraid that they would be hurt during clashes with police. Some were quite happy to see women demonstrating as long as it wasn't their women. Others again wanted women to be involved but only under direction from and consultation with the men, and objected to them taking their own decisions. For over a hundred years, miners had not worked with women and many still had a patronising manner towards them. For some men, the amount of ef-fort women put into the strike changed those attitudes, but others couldn't cope; some marriages broke up and families were split. Some pit deputies had to keep working to enable the pit to be kept open, and had to pass family members on the picket line.

Non-working miners were free to participate in strike activities, but women also had homes to run and children to care for. One of the results of the women's involvement was that for the first time, men were having to look after the children. Another was that positions in the home were reversed with the wife becoming the breadwinner. Most jobs, however, were part-time and poorly paid so, though the money went a little way towards providing for the family, it was by no means sufficient. Working wives were often in a worse position than others because banks and hire purchase companies were less sympathetic when even a tiny wage was coming into the house.

Some building societies froze mortgage payments, others were not so compassionate. Savings were non-existent and insurance policies had to be cashed in. For these women it must have seemed that not only the government and the police force were against them, but they also had to fight with those closer to home. People who were ac-tive during the strike were subjected to attacks - windows broken, cars sprayed with paint, washing burnt on the line and abusive phone calls received, One woman, whose husband was in prison for strike activities had her name and phone number written on a pub wall was continually pestered till it was found where the nuisance calls were coming from and men from the strike centre went and removed the offensive graffiti.

Living conditions were grim. Pensioners who were ex-miners were refused coal and had to rely on gifts of wood and coal from the small seams that the men occasionally found to work. People sat wrapped in blankets round empty grates. If firewood was scarce, anything that would burn was utilised - clothes, old shoes, or home made bri-quettes made out of coal dust. Young couples were having to go back to their parents homes because they had no way of keeping the children warm. As the strike intensi-fied, villages were turned into armed camps, and innocent people were arrested outside their own houses. Talk of police shortages disappeared as forces from all over the country were brought in to defeat the miners. Policemen were everywhere, men and women were stopped on the public highway and refused permission to go about their lawful business. Breach of the peace offences, which normally carried a twenty pound fine, suddenly rose to three to four hundred pounds. Offenders were sent to the sheriff court instead of being dealt with by a local JP. Phones at strike centres were tapped,

Fine suddenly rose to between three and four hundred pounds. Others were sent to the sheriff court instead of being dealt with by a local JP. Phones at strike centres were tapped and when a woman was injured during a picket at Coal Board headquarters the police refused to press charges because it wasn't an official union demonstration, just a 'bunch of women.' A mass picket was organised at Polkemmet Colliery on February 14th and women and children came from all over the country. So did the police. They refused to let the buses near the pit so women had to walk miles in the snow . Police threatened to arrest one woman for banging a tambourine and shouting 'scab.' Women with prams were pushed aside while police chased men over the fields. Much of the bitterness towards the government focused on the steel plant at Ravenscraig, where Yuill and Dodds, a local haulage firm were employed to run imported coal. Our Dalkeith correspondent described one experience.

'The courage shown by the women that morning amazed me. Some of the really quiet women went that day even though they knew how dangerous and menacing the men had said it was. They showed a kind of inner strength and God knows, we needed it. When we saw the amount of police and horsemen, there were at least five police for each miner, it was so sad , so disillusioning.' [11]

Bilston Glen returned to work a week after the strike ended with pipes playing 'Scotland the Brave' and with women in the procession. The sacked men marched at the front carrying the union banner and at the pit gates, the manager tried to take it from them. By the time the strike ended, two hundred and six Scottish miners had been sacked and were refused their jobs back even when Industrial Relations Tribunals found in their favour. A year later over five hundred sacked men throughout Britain were still out of work. They lost their redundancy, their pension rights and their houses. Martha MacCallum's husband took part in a sit in down the pit and was fired, despite nearly twenty years service. He won an unfair dismissal case after five years but was never reinstated. Scotland had only half as many miners as the rest of Britain but four times as many dismissals, and two years after the strike ended, women's groups were still raising money for sacked miners families.

The end of the strike had meant even greater hardship. Bills and arrears which had been held in abeyance, began to flood in, arrears of rent and other payments had to be made up and as soon as work began again, creditors demanded payment. Immediately the strike ended all families given loans by Strathclyde Region received demands for repayment and the question of the loans became the centre of a legal storm. Strathclyde's Director of Social Work faced the possibility of being made personally responsible for around £190,000, the sum total of the loans, because the Auditor General questioned their legal status. [12]

The extent of the debt problem is also demonstrated by a news item in The Dunfermline Press in January 1987. Fife Council were considering calling in debt collectors to recoup loans given to mining families. More than a million pounds had been paid out to two thousand one hundred and fifty five families. Though the majority of people were paying instalments, this was only one debt among others, and almost two thirds of the amount was still outstanding. In addition, the report said there had been problems with loan sharks, a number of marriages had broken up and men had left the area to find work.

Women were reluctant to go back to their old way of life. During the strike they had experienced a new kind of social life, meeting together as women, and new and enduring friendships were made. Everyone was glad that the long struggle was over but sad too, in a way, because they realised that they would never again have that closeness and cameraderie, the sense of everyone sticking together.

Women wanted to keep their solidarity together somehow. The strike had provided an opportunity for them to make their voices heard and they kept it going even after the leaders had decided to call a halt. More importantly, women became aware of their own potential power in politics. They joined forces with nuclear disarmers, joined the cause of black miners in Namibia who provided uranium for British Nuclear Fuels and with Pacific Islanders whose homes were used for testing nuclear weapons that were later deployed at Greenham and Faslane. Two women from the Greenham peace camp were invited to speak at the Miners Gala in Edinburgh, and it must have been strange to see women on a traditional all-male platform. Some of the women at the base came from mining communities, but they were at Greenham from choice. Miners wives didn't have any choice.

Women Against Pit Closures opposed nuclear energy, not just for the sake of jobs but because of the fear of nuclear accident. Britain was going down the costly road of nuclear energy, though a similar project in the United States had been abandoned because of doubts about its safety. To realise the validity of the fear, one only has to think of Chernobyl and the hospitals full of children with leukaemia because of nuclear testing in the Russian Arctic. The claim of necessary investment in and expansion of nuclear power was in doubt because the Scottish electricity grid had a surplus which was keeping English customers free from power cuts during the strike.

In recognition of their contribution, women were allowed to become associate members of the Scottish National Union of Mineworkers and it is only now, over seventy years since universal women's suffrage was introduced, that women in Scotland are achieving a measurable degree of democratic representation.

CHAPTER THIRTEEN

IT'S OUR HISTORY - THEY'VE GOT TO GET IT RIGHT

There are still a few pit-head lassies about. Some are shy about being interviewed because old prejudices against them are remembered, but enough stories remain to explode once and for all the myth that they belonged to a kind of sub-culture, a suitable subject only of historical and intellectual curiosity.

These women have a pride in their past. Working at the pit head made them tough but it didn't brutalise them. They had a rough and ready friendly relationship with the miners, came from respectable working class homes and given the chance, could and did make a success of their lives. This is not measured in terms of worldly wealth, though that was achieved too, but by less material standards. Whether alone or surrounded by several generations of extended families, the qualities they brought to life shine through. Honesty, loyalty to family, friends and employers, an enormous sense of humour and above all a determination to enjoy life, to make the most of what it brings. What their early experiences gave them was an ability to cope with whatever life threw at them.

*The conveyor belt is stopped long enough for these girls to be photographed
at the Michael Colliery picking tables*

BARBARA MARSHALL

Barbara celebrated her one hundredth birthday in August , 2000, surrounded by one hundred and thirty members of five generations of her family. As the oldest resident of Cowdenbeath her birthday caused quite a splash with a visit from Alistair Darling, the Minister of Pensions and from the Lord Lieutenant of Fife, who delivered a telegram from the Queen. Barbara shares a birthday month with the Queen Mother, but that is the only thing they have in common. Born in Dunfermline, her father and four brothers were all miners and Barbara left school at fourteen to start work at Fordell Pit.

' I was one of twelve children and remember moving from Inverkeithing to Fordell and my mother enrolling me at Mossgreen School; gas mantles, paraffin lamps and outside toilets and carrying the water into the house from outside. Fordell only had one shop. We had Sunday School trips, picnics to Fordell Lodge. We went in hay carts all dressed up with ribbons and things. Once when we got to Coaledge, one of the horses fell down dead in the shafts. The church was very important to us. I've been a life long member, attending Crossgates and Hill of Beath. The Earl and Countess of Buckingham used to come to Fordell for the Show. Their son was called Lord Hobart. My father used to drive the pug and they got a new one called Lord Hobart. One year they said 'Three cheers for Lord Hobart' and the kids all said 'Three cheers for the pug.'

I started work straight from school and did everything on the pit head. I can't remember how many girls worked there but there were two or three tables for different types of coal, and waggons for every different lie. They got weighed further down and all went out on different lines . We had to set the waggons, climb up and sort the coal so it wouldn't fall off. We started at six in the morning and worked till two. Men worked all shifts but the girls just worked day shift . We took the redd off the coal with a wee pick and flung it aside, the rest went on the table. Some of the hutches came up the pit and they weren't weighed because they thought there was too much dirt in them. Some girls were chosen to pick the worst of the dirt out and the men didn't like it but it was the girls' job. Then the waggon went through to the tumbler and the coal came on to the tables. It was very noisy. You couldn't hear your own voice. We got one and three a day. There was a pit head gaffer and a table gaffer. He had to pick a girl to pick stones out of the churly table and she got one and fivepence.

I left school on the Friday and started on the Monday. My mother and father didn't want me to go. Father said, 'No girl of mine is going to work on the pit head' but I went. I was never down the pit but did plenty work on the pit head, put hutches onto the cage, pulled them up the cage and put them through the tumblers. The coal went down on to the tables then to the waggons to be delivered to different places. I never wore trousers in my life, we had tackety boots, long skirts and jumpers and a shawl over our heads to keep the dust out of our hair. When you finished at two o'clock, you put on a clean apron to go home. You changed your pinny and washed your hair every day because the coal dust got everywhere.

My brother was wounded in the war, he was in the Black Watch and I remember my mother going to Manchester when he was wounded. But he came back and started in the Alice Pit and was six weeks off his wedding when he died. He was only twenty four. My husband was killed in 1959 and I had five of a family but you just have to take everything as it comes. Long ago we were all the same, no-one had money. Just after we were married, my husband was ill for five years and I took in washing and knitting and made rag rugs, anything that would make an honest shilling and we brought up our kids to the best of our ability. We started off in a single end in Broad Street but it fell down so we went to Woodside then to Maxwell Crescent and we've been there for fifty one years.

It wasn't an easy life but I think we were happier then. There was a picture house in Crossgates, the Drome, it didn't have fancy seats, just chairs. There was a picture house in Cowdenbeath too and the Palais de Danse and Jock McGin's dance hall. We went to Co-operative Hall dances and we went to the Opera House in Dunfermline. I remember when the talkies started, it was a great excitement after the silent films. There was a change of pictures Monday, Wednesday and Friday. I enjoyed my life, had a happy life and couldn't wish for anything better.'

No 9 Pit Cowdenbeath c1910

ANN EDEN

I was born in August 1919, and shortly before my fourteenth birthday, I started work at Brighills Colliery alongside my sister Josephine. Josie wanted to be a school teacher but our father insisted she leave school like everyone else and get a job in the pit. My first job was in the lamp cabin where the miner's lamps were stored. Coming on shift they shouted out their numbers, I gave them out the lamps and then collected them in after the end of the day's work. Clanny carbide lamps had to be filled with naptha and lamps with batteries had to be charged. They sat in little porcelain dishes and my dungarees were riddled with holes from spilled acid. Dungarees cost half a crown a pair and that was very expensive, a quarter of my weekly wage of ten shillings. When I got my pay, I had to pay 5/8 for my mother's rent and I got two shillings pocket money.

The work was long and hard. The day began with the horn at the Jenny Grey pit blowing at five fifteen a.m. That was the signal to get up. Then we had a cup of tea and a bit of toast made against the ribs of the grate or a piece and jam. We took a couple of slices of bread and a tin flask of tea. We would watch the men hiding their cigarettes and tobacco before they went down the pit and sometimes the girls would pinch them and have a smoke but the men got wise and changed their hiding place. Later, when the baths came, we had a thermos flask and a wee case to keep our pieces in. We had to be careful or the rats would get them, there was only a shelf in the bothy for them. At nine o'clock we went in to the tables to pick stones from the coal.

The coal came down the tumbler on to a shaker, we picked out stones and rubbish and used picks to break stones from the coal. There were five picking tables, the worst was for anthracite coal, it was very bright and sharp and cut our fingers like razors and the dust covered everything like a blanket. Other jobs included working on the pins, a kind of tally system. Each hutch full of coal had a peg identifying the miner and the section of the pit it came from, so a check could be made on individual production. At two o'clock when the morning shift came up, the girls went to the pit yards to collect pit props and straps, as many as five hundred of each. These were built up in piles in the yard so high that usually we had to climb up to throw the wood down. The girls would pick up five six-foot straps at a time and then lay them out in rows for the men to take down the pit. We worked every second Saturday till one o'clock and only ever got a rest from work if there was an overwind, that is when the waggon went right up to the pulley wheels. Accidents were common, my sister Alice had her middle finger nearly severed. She worked on the tumblers, put the hutches in and pulled the lever and the coal was emptied on to the shaker. Her finger was caught but she got it sewn back on again.

Later on, I worked at the back of the pit where full hutches came from the pit bottom and empty ones were sent down. The cages were double deckers, holding two hutches and I had to operate the points to move waggons from one rail to another. If waggons came off the rails, the girls had to manhandle them back on again. Our shift ended at three fifteen and before pit baths came in to existence, we tried to clean our faces as best we could before going home. We didn't have hot water and girls had to wait till the men got washed first, then the boys. When the pit baths opened, men were catered for on the ground floor while upstairs, the women were provided with showers and big basins for washing their hair. Downstairs there were special brushes to clean the worst of the coal dirt from our shoes, then we'd go upstairs to the locker room with our dirty clothes, strip into the showers and dress in our outdoor clothes in the "clean room."

The provision of pit head baths revolutionised the homes of mining families, it made life much easier, but many people preferred the old ways. When the council began building homes to take the place of the old miners rows, my mother refused one, and chose an old house instead with one toilet and wash house shared by three families. My mother had twenty children, including three sets of twins but only twelve of them lived to be adults. Seven of them were younger than me and the problems of rearing such a large family must have been phenomenal, but to us it was just normal. My father worked in the garden and looked after the quoits pitch. He was blinded in the pit and got a lump sum of £200.00 and a pension of ten shillings a week. I remember during the General Strike in 1926, I used to go and see my sister Daisy who worked in the Minto Hotel in Lochgelly. The hotel had to feed the army of policemen brought in to control the miners and Daisy would smuggle out food to us younger ones. I can also remember seeing the glass sided hearse and the horses with black plumes going down the Eliza Brae to the cemetery.

But it's not the bad times we remember. Like everyone else, it's the happiness and the simple life. After work, there were keep fit and cookery classes, and we went to the pictures in Lochgelly for two pence and carried on with the boys. Saturdays saw the "shillingy dash" to Edinburgh when all the youngsters piled into the train from Cardenden to Edinburgh. We went to the Kings Theatre and had our photos taken at Jeromes in Leith Road. This was only a brief escape, the only way out was to get married. But girls did escape not just from the work but from the limited expectations of life style and wealth. One of my sisters became lady's maid to a countess and my sister Bella, who like me started work at the pit head when she was fourteen, married a miner and together they achieved the kind of life that would be envied by many. Eventually working for the United Nations, they travelled the world, were wealthy and successful and their grandchildren went to Cambridge University.

There must have been lots of other girls like Bella but who didn't get a chance. I worked for eight years in the pit before I got married. My husband was a winding engine man and we lived in Cumnock but after he died of a heart attack, I went to my sister in Chessington and a life as far as possible removed from mining. I worked in London for the John Lewis Partnership, looking after the linen for their restaurants. With my second husband I came home to Fife after we retired.

Donald Rose Brickworks Aberhill Methil

1930 Brighills Josie Bernard on left

GRACE MACKINNON

I was fifteen when I went to work in the Michael Colliery. I was in service but was between jobs when the war began in 1939 and had to get a job. I remember the bombs falling in a field close to where we were working and when the air raid sounded, we went down a tunnel into the shelter which had been bored out of solid rock in the cliff side. Only a few men worked on the pit head, mostly older men or those who were exempt from war work, but lots of women and girls of all ages. Many of the older women there had worked on the picking tables for most of their lives but the young girls were glad to leave and join the services. Picking was dirty and unpleasant, and coal dust and the bitter cold got everywhere in spite of dungarees, big jerseys, scarves and mittens.

The boss had a wooden leg and above the noise of the machinery we could hear him stomping along the verandah above us. Because of the noise we couldn't talk so communicated by sign language. As the youngest recruit, it was my job to go the shop at break time and often this took so long that it was time to go back to work before I got back, but if I was lucky I was given a piece of chocolate for my efforts.

Among the coal and stones that came up from below were sometimes bits of sleepers and old broken pit props, some of which were laid aside to take home. Smaller pieces went on the fire where billy cans were boiled for piece time. Sometimes there were

Glencraig Pit lassies 1927

less pleasant things in the hutches, men would put dead rats in among the coal to frighten us and fleas got into our clothes and multiplied in the clothes lockers. Day-shift was from six till two thirty and back shift from twelve thirty till ten. In winter we went to work in the dark and came home in the dark. We had to take the stones and dirt out of the coal coming up and when we were busy the big stones had to be put aside till the coal waggons stopped coming for a time. Then they were split with hammer and pick and the coal and stone separated, each going into its own waggon.

I came from a mining family, but as well as mining, East Fife had linen weaving, paper making, bottle works and steel works. I was quite happy to leave the pit head as soon as I was old enough to join the army, but I did return to the pits afterwards, working in the Bevan Boys canteen at Muiredge.

MARGARET RODGER

My dad was a miner, he worked in the Victoria Pit and I started work at the Michael Colliery when I was fifteen. Before that, I'd been at Wemyss Castle for a year but I could earn two shillings a week more in the pit and I liked it better than being in service. I was born in September 1917 and there was seven children in the family. With my sisters, I'd walk from West Wemyss and sometimes when the sea was rough we would climb over the cemetery wall instead of going round by the shore. There were about fifty five girls at the Michael and though it was hard work, we still enjoyed ourselves. During break time one of the women would play a mouth organ and we'd dance.

I worked on the picking tables with the men. They threw down huge lumps of coal for the girls to separate the stone from the coal with picks, then we had to break up the stones so they were small enough to go through the wire mesh onto the conveyor belt below. We were supposed to start work at six and finish at two, but we often began at five because we had a good boss and would do anything to please him. When I put a pick through my toe, I didn't complain because he might get into trouble. There was no protective footwear or overalls, we mostly wore trousers and a jersey because we couldn't afford dungarees. By the end of the day, our skin and hair were ingrained with coal dust and we didn't have hot water.

Our bathroom consisted of half a beer barrel filled with hot water from the kettle. The house had two rooms and a living room with set in beds, our brother had one and us four girls shared the other. We slept top to tail. My mother was so small she had to stand on a chair to do the washing.

For entertainment, there was dancing in the Masonic hall for sixpence or in the Bowling Green dance hall in Methil, but at two shillings that was too dear for a lot of us and we had the choice of going to the dancing or buying a sixpenny packet of five Woodbine cigarettes. Buckhaven was the big city for us. West Wemyss consisted of five pubs, a clock and a cemetery, with a population of about one hundred people plus a policeman but it had its gala day with races and pipe bands. The Post Office doubled up as a pub and me and my sister used to be sent with a jug to collect beer for our father when he was on back shift.

All the girls had chores to do when we got home, but our brother, he was the only boy, was a spoilt brat, he would sit back like a prince while his shoes were cleaned and shirts ironed. Though he was used to having his own way, when it came to getting a job, he had to go down the pit like the rest of the family. Sometimes we had to take our picks to the smiddy to get sharpened, and father kept his caps and the strum that was used for blasting the coal, on a shelf in the kitchen. We bairns were forbidden to touch them. My father was a fisherman in his spare time, with his own boat and one of my best memories is of him taking his accordion out in the boat and the sound of his music floating cross the water.

Life was better in those days, there was no drugs or thieving and people were tough because we had to be. We had to take everything life threw at us. I've smoked since I was sixteen and have had nineteen operations for cancer but I'm a survivor.

Loganlea Colliery pit head workers Packie McCole, Mick McGarvie and Dan McCole with Sarah Thomson the last female pit worker in Lanarkshire

MARGARET WRIGHT

I was born in Lindsay Square in Methil, in June 1923, the only one of eleven children to be born in Fife. My family came from Blantyre and my mother didn't like Fife but they had to come here for there was no work in Blantyre. I left school at 14 and began work the next week in the Lochhead Pit in Kirkcaldy. To be at work by six, I had to get up at four, leave home at half-past, catch the bus at quarter to five then have a half hour's walk to reach the pit. Other girls from round about worked at the same pit, but they were on a different shift, so I'd run up the road to meet other miners for company in the dark mornings. The back shift was from two thirty to ten and you were home by eleven. On day shift the miners came up the pit at one o'clock and we had to clear up and prepare for the next shift.

 I swore I wouldn't stick it, you were always dirty, your skin and hair, and I left after a year and a half. I went into service but couldn't stand the loneliness and went back to the pit. I got my job back because I'd been a good worker but still swore I wouldn't make it my life and got a job in the Deaconess Hospital in Edinburgh. I was there when the war started and remember the sirens going off, I was in Princes Street at the time. We had to put all the beds in the centre of the ward and then we hid in the fruit cellar. That was a bonus because we didn't get much fruit. Then I went home and into the steelworks, making Bren guns at Kirklands in Leven and I got married when I was eighteen and a half.

Lassies wouldn't be in the pits if they could get a better job, but the pay was good, fifteen shillings at that time (1937). We stood for hours at the tables, the tubs came up and the coals came down the chute onto the picking tables. There were different tables for different sizes of coal. On the biggest, you had to climb up onto the table and pick and pick till you got the stones out. You moved round the table, changed places, wore gloves if you could afford them, but not many could. You were always dirty, skin and hair, your whole body as well as your hands and you had to have a bath every day if your mother could afford it.

 It was a hard time. My sister went to work in the Michael after her marriage broke up and I helped to look after her children. The Michael employed a lot of women but the Lochhead had only about twenty. There were no accidents among the women as far as I can recall, but two men working on power cables were electrocuted when someone switched on the electricity. One landed on the picking table with blood running from his finger tips.

Like everyone else, we worked on bread and jam, sometimes bread and marge. I'd tell my mother to give me marge and two pence for crisps and I'd spend the money on Woodbines. We had one meal a day after work, but no luxuries. On Saturdays, day shift ended at one thirty and at tea break we'd spend three pence on toffee. Pocket money was a shilling a week- for six days work - but it was amazing what that shilling could do. We made our own entertainment, had midnight balls with old time dancing at the Methilhill Institute which cost sixpence. They began at four minutes past midnight on a Sunday night and if we were on day shift, we'd to leave at ten to four to change into working clothes, and then be falling asleep over the tables and have the foreman shouting at us.

On Friday nights we went to the Palace Picture House in Methil, which cost two pence, then we'd have a fish supper for three pence and have a pennyworth of sweets. We kept back sixpence for the dancing but on the back shift we just spent it. During the war we had talent competitions to raise money for comforts for the troops.

It was a hard life but people were friendly and helped each other. Miners clung to one another because everyone was in the same boat. Poverty was a way of life, but so also was pride. Our shoes were polished but they had cardboard in them when the soles were worn through. I was interviewed for a job in Wemyss Castle, and was offered five shillings a week to work all hours of the day and night when guests, which included royalty were in residence. As well as working eighteen hours a day, I was expected to buy my own uniform. My mother refused to let me go, and its not surprising that girls chose to work at the pit head rather than more elegant slavery.

The church played little part in our lives. Children went to the Gospel Hall and the Salvation Army, because they had picnic trips with a free bag of buns and you took your tinnie for lemonade. There was always an upsurge in membership as trip time drew near. My father started work when he was eleven and he and three of my brothers died of lung cancer but when he retired, all there was to show for it was a certificate which said he had given fifty years of his life to the pit.

After my husband died, I was left with a half pension of £23.00 a week so had to find a job and for twenty years I was nurse-housekeeper to a disabled man. I travelled the world with him, cruises on the Canberra, Spain every year, Italy, Bulgaria, but when I was young I went tattie picking and picked stones from farmers' fields. I enjoyed working at the pit but left with no regrets and filled with determination that my children would never have to go through what I did. Some people looked on pit head lassies as the lowest of the low but we did an honest day's work for an honest day's pay and we shouldn't be ashamed of it.

JOHAN CAIRNS

The first job I had was at the Jenny Grey, taking coal in hutches out to the bin and I was so wee they couldn't see me at the back of the hutch. That was just after I left school in January 1937, I was fourteen. Then I was at the picking tables but I wasn't long there. I did every job there was to do at the pit head. When the men below put the coal into the hutches, they put their pin on. At the top of the creeper was the pin box and you had to stand there and take the pins off. The weighman checked the number and the weight and that's how the miner got paid.

My next job was the switches. The tumblers dropped the coal onto the picking tables below and the cleaned coal went into the waggons below that again. The empty hutches went right round and came in the back of the pit again, they pushed the full ones out. It was like a conveyor belt system, it worked in a circle. The coal stopped coming up at one o'clock and the pit head had to be cleaned till it was nearly spotless. There was no coal came up on the back shift. In the summertime, when the coal wasn't being sold, it was taken out and binged. At that time, we had summers so no-one was buying and it was built up into piles ready for when it was needed in the winter. Then they employed men to fill hutches from the bing and they were brought up on a hoist.

We started at six, stopped for twenty minutes at nine for a cup of tea, had a toilet break at twelve, lunch break from one till half past and finished at three. I worked every second Saturday, cleaning the offices, you got three shillings for a Saturday shift. At that time, men were going home with two pounds. There were about fifteen to twenty girls and four picking tables. No men worked on the pit head except for maintenance. When I first started there were horses, ponies underground, they used to bring them up on Friday and take them down again on Sunday. You could hear them kicking against the cage. Some people thought ponies in the pit were blind but they weren't and they were well treated, the men were aye feeding them. They had a wee field of their own.

The Jenny Grey had two shafts, a deep one and a shallow one, it was about fourteen feet. We used to shout down to the men to see if they wanted anything from the shop. I was there for six years till I got married. My dad belonged to Nairn, his father was a fisherman and he was a plasterer to trade but the only job he could get in Fife was in the pit. He worked for twenty years at the Minto. There was a big accident at the pit and some men were killed. That day he was ill, but he had to go down because he was the ambulance man and when he saw what it was like he never went back. My son was at the pit head for a while but we're not a mining family.

My mother's family were carpenters and joiners. There were six of us and my husband came from a family of twelve. They were miners, they came from Rosewell to Lochgelly. My man was in the pit till he went to the army and he went back after the war. Underground miners were exempt but he joined up a fortnight before the war started. His only injury was a broken leg from playing football but he was an antitank gunner and went right into Berlin. He was with the army that liberated Belsen, he got leave after that and used to have nightmares. It made him hard, he didn't have much sympathy for the bairns' cuts and bruises after that.

He used to work in The Jenny Grey and I'd get him up the pit. I had to ring the bell for the winding engine man to bring the cage up. I went down the pit twice and was surprised because it was like a big cave, all whitewashed and you could see all the railway lines going off in different directions. Its not stuffy in the main parts but it would have been in the narrow seams. Sometimes they were only eighteen inches deep. The men didn't get the money they deserved for that work. Neither did we, but there wasn't a standard pay. We got two and six but in Brighills it was one and eleven pence ha'penny.

On back shift or night shift, there'd be one man in charge. He'd maybe need four or six men and would be told how much he could offer. Some paid more than others. When we got married my man was getting six and six a day but he got nine and nine pence on night shift doing the same work. During the war, I used to go along to the pit and get coal. I wasn't entitled to free coal because Chick had left, but the men would fill a sandbag for us and the manager would turn a blind eye and sometimes make sure I got two bags.

It was the Lochgelly Iron and Coal Company then and they had a brick works, too. I'd work in the Jenny Grey till three then get a lift out to the brick works on the pug engine and work for two hours for nothing. My pal's two sisters worked there and we'd go and help them. You didn't get taken on at the brick works till you were eighteen and the manager wanted us to leave the pit and work there, but I didn't go. I wouldn't leave the Jenny Grey. We had quite a good life there with a social club and there used to be a hall in the next street where we had dances nearly every Friday night. You used to wear long frocks and white ankle socks and white shoes. My mother was a dressmaker so we got a new frock every other week. Material cost about sixpence a yard, socks were sixpence and shoes eleven pence ha'penny a pair. We had balls, too, they began at ten and finished at five, we came home in time to change our clothes ready for work. We never thought anything about it.

I never stopped working even when I was married for my mother had a late bairn, he was only three months older than my first one and including him, I had four bairns under four year old. You change your life when you have bairns, go from an eight hour day to a twenty four hour one. We had a boiler and after finishing the washing, you filled it up again and let the fire go out till it was cool enough for the bairns to be bathed in. I aye threatened to keep the fire on.

The pit head lassies all got on well enough but some of them wouldn't leave the tables, they were frightened to try other work because there was more responsibility. There was a thing we called the snibble, an iron bar with a loop on the end where you gripped it and you had to catch the wheel of the tub to stop it. The only thing I liked at the table was the shovelling. The old boy who looked after the machinery was supposed to be helping and he picked up the wee axe head we used for splitting the redd from the coal and split my finger with it. His name was John Knox but I cried him everything but a Christian.

Accidents weren't common. In six years, one laddie of fifteen was killed and a man had a heart attack. That was on one of my Saturday shifts. I went to the ambulance room because I had to clean it and when I opened the door I saw a big pair of pit boots facing me. I got pushed outside but then I was asked to go and tell his people he had died. There was no-one else to do it.

In 1934, I think it was, lightning struck the big chimney and knocked the side right out of it. We thought we were going to get a week off work and were told to go and sign on the dole but they rigged it up and we only got a half day off . The chimney was taken down and built up by steeplejacks and I climbed up the inside of the flew chimney. Nobody dares me to do anything, they said I couldn't do it but I did. The steeplejack was at my back, of course.

When I retired from my job at the dockyard, I went to Australia to Victoria, and my cousin took me to see the mines there, they were all surface mines and the coal is dark brown, not black. There was a tower with two hundred steps where you could see over all the work. I didn't like that much, I was glad to get down. I was a catering assistant in the dockyard, with a snack bar for the apprentices. Before that I was a home help.

I remember during the strike in 1926 the Jenny Grey was on strike and there were soldiers with guns. We got a thumping from my mother for standing on top of the bing and shouting at them. We went to Lochgelly East School then, it was where the Centre is now, and there was no shortage of jobs in the pit when you left.

I liked the pit head. When you finished your day's work, there was no-one at your back; every one had their job to do and when it was done and everything cleaned up, that was it. It was a dirty job, I wore dungarees and five jerseys for the cold. I got up at 5.45, left the house at 5.55 in time to start work at six. My jerseys came on and off in a oner. Some time ago there was a photo in the library which was supposed to be the Jenny Grey in the thirties and the girls were all wearing long skirts and aprons and shawls round their heads. I complained and got the other women who worked alongside me to do the same. It's our history. They've got to get it right.

JEAN GRAHAM

Jean is unique for several reasons. She is one of the last few women to work on the pit head in Scotland and one of the even fewer number of women this century whose entire working lives were spent in the mining industry. She also did jobs that were normally the preserve of men, though needless to say, she didn't get men's wages.

'I was born in South Street Lochgelly and lived in the town all my life. When I left school first I got a job cleaning and polishing for a woman whose family were all working. That was considered a high class job but I only got five shillings a week, so I started on the picking tables at 1/11 a day. I started work at the Brighills Minto pit in 1936. There were no baths then and we were covered in stour and when I got home I was so tired and sore all over I'd go ben the room lie on the rug in front of the fire and have to be wakened up to get washed and go to bed. We worked six days a week and had a week's holiday without pay. The picking tables were downstairs and after a bit I got put on to the back of the pit where all the hutches were.

They went into the tumblers, you pulled a lever and the coal went down a chute onto the picking tables. At the back of the tumblers, the fellows pushed the empty one out and you had to pull it away round so it went up what was called a creeper, a kind of chain that kept the hutches moving, pulled them to the pit cage ready to go back down again. A snibble was a piece of iron, a half-circle to keep the hutches on the cage. I used to get them from the old hutch menders who repaired the old wooden hutches before the metal ones came in.

At the start of the war all the men were taken away to the pit so I had to go to the front of the pit, to pull the full hutches off, put the empty ones back on and put them back down the pit. I've put men down too and took them up again in the cage. You pulled a lever and the message went to the engine man and he lowered the cage. I was fourteen years there at the front of that pit and when I look back, I often see men I used to work with and they say, "I don't know how you done that" and I often wonder myself. We were a happy crowd, we used to go to the Institute dancing on a Thursday, it was three pence to get in. All the pit head girls used to go there but as time went on they all got married and there were only three or four of us left and we were there till the pit closed down. After the foreman at the picking tables took ill, they had no-one to take his place. That's when all the young ones started to come in and they were a rough crowd and I was asked to take over. I hesitated a bit but eventually I took over and they were only a couple of months there and they got put down the pit so you knew you only had to suffer them for a wee while, but they were nothing to the women at the picking tables.

And the tables, they revolved and it was clanging shaking metal noise all the time, like a treadmill. The coal and stones came down this shaker and you had to pick all the stones out, you had to break the big stones with picks or seven pound hammers. The girls used to climb on to the moving table to heave off big stones that they couldn't break, there was a knack to it but once I jumped up and my leg slipped through

Pit head women, Lanarkshire, 1920s
Women workers at screening plant No 1 Pit, Bothwellhaugh

and I just managed to get it free before it was trapped. I had sixteen stitches in it. One girl dropped a lump of coal on her foot and got blood poisoning .In winter time if you didn't have gloves, your hands would stick to the iron and the frosty wind from the shaft was bitter. Your hands would be bleeding with hacks you'd rub them with oil at night and they'd be sore when you put them into hot water. You had to suffer the noise from the tables from the minute you started to the time you finished. You couldn't speak, the tables were about a yard wide and you used sign language. And the stour was terrible. I'm deaf in one ear and I got turned down for compensation.

I was glad when the pit closed. I was getting too old in my forties then, I'd been there thirty three years. I got a watch with my name inscribed on it, and we had a tea with the old miners and some of the officials of The Coal Board. There were only three women left then, we still look after each other. We were the last pit lassies in Scotland, in 1967 that was, August or September, I think. I've got a scroll that I got from Lord Robens, he was the head of the Coal Board at the time.

I wasn't called a fore woman but was cried the gaffer at the tables. There was a scheme where laddies had to come and do table work before they went down the pit. Our under manager he was the head of it and I had to go to him to get lines signed certifying that I was their boss. I did the drawing off at the front of the pit for 14 years including the war years and I remember doing Sunday shifts, they were called Victory shifts, there was always a full turn out. A lot of miners, those on the pit head were called up but underground workers were exempt.

There were eight of us, but three brothers were killed in the war and two that worked in the pit died of pneumonoconiosis. My father was a miner too. We enjoyed our work and had money in our pockets. I got 2/3 when I started at the front of the pit then it began to rise. There wasn't much choice, it was either service or factory or down the pit. Life was really hard when you had no baths. My mother had a boiler and after the washing was done, she'd put more water on to beat and we'd have a bath in this boiler. Long ago, your father had his bath in a wooden tub. My mother died in 1938, the year before the war.

We'd get the quarter past five bus in the morning but some of the laddies who were pals of mine would walk so I'd walk down the road with them. Sometimes in the pouring rain, you'd be soaked before you started. When the baths came, it was rare. I just worked day shift. but if there was a breakdown in the pit, they'd ask you to lie on and sometimes it was six o'clock before you got home. I remember once there was a big breakdown and I didn't get home till ten o'clock at night - that was from quarter past five in the morning, and you had to get up for your work the next morning.

It was a hard life, slave labour really, for peanuts and we were doing a man's job but getting women's pay. Equal rights? That was one place that should have had equal rights. I was doing a man's job , drawing off at the front of the pit, it was a man doing the job before he went to the war.

I don't agree with equality, there's a lot of jobs women can't do, but we should have had the same wages. I was gaffer, over young laddies and older men who weren't fit

to work underground. I was their boss but they but they got more money than me.
Brighills should have been closed two years before it did, but it was kept going. The
pit was at the bottom of Eliza Brae, there were rows of pit houses there too. I wouldn't
say we loved our job but we were quite happy in our work. We wore boiler suits and
dust caps, turban kind of things. The Coal Board issued us with clothes but we had to
supply our own footwear. I had bad feet because during the war, we couldn't get shoes
and I used to kick the snecks down, they were round bits of iron that kept the hutches
in position in the cage. You knocked them down with you feet and half the time
there was no side in my shoe, I was kicking it with my bare foot. But we were fit, we
had no health problems. Chrissie smoked like a chimney all her life and doesn't even
have a cough. Every day the lassies would wash their hair and go home with it wet,
summer and winter, and never had a cold. I kept my hair covered like a nun.
When the baths came, I was asked to clean the baths for a time till they got a new
cleaner and I ended up doing that for years as well as my own work. Some women
from Brighills had no baths in their houses and they'd come along for a bath on a
Thursday. Young ones today don't know they're living. You'd never know now there
were ever pits there. When we finished work, the papers came but we didn't want a
fuss, we just wanted to get washed and get away home. We didn't realise we were
making history.

GLENCRAIG PIT. 1925

CHAPTER FOURTEEN

WOMEN AND MINING TODAY

When Helen Crawfurd died in 1954, the mines had been nationalised, and with the National Health Service, the country was well on the way to eradicating many of the problems of ill health and malnutrition that she had fought against. The employment of women remained a bone of contention, though rather smaller than it had been. The years 1939 - 45 witnessed a sharp increase in the number of female mining employees though it was not till 1943 that uniformity of wages was introduced. Numbers dwindled quickly after the war and by the 1950s, when women pit head workers left or were made redundant, they were not replaced. Disabled miners were given preference in surface jobs and elderly miners were engaged rather than women. Others were given jobs as canteen assistants or switchboard operators. At the beginning of the decade, there were less than a thousand women working in collieries and, in 1954, Margaret Herbison, Labour Member for Lanarkshire suggested that no further recruiting be allowed. Changes in social and economic circumstances made it possible for girls to travel to alternate work in factories, shops and offices.

The 1954 act was the last major mining legislation to deal with women's employment in the industry, though an act in 1975 permitted their employment in disused mines and 'occasionally in active mines' as long as their jobs did not take them underground for a significant proportion of time. This allowed women doctors and nurses to attend accident victims underground when necessary.

One of these nurses was Elsie Brodie who worked with the Coal Board for three years in the seventies:

' I was a district nurse and once I brought up my family I was looking for something to do, but had hurt my back at work so wanted a non-lifting job. I'd been working with an agency doing relief work in industry when the Coal Board advertised for a relief nurse for the collieries . For six months I did relief work in mines around Fife and the Lothians, then Solsgirth mine had a vacancy so I applied and got the job.

Basically what I did for the next three years was to look after the health of miners. We had a medical centre as well as a casualty centre. I worked nine till five and round the clock we had medical room attendants who worked either back shift or night shift, providing twenty four hour cover. If we weren't there, the bath attendants all had first aid certificates. Most of the minor injuries were treated at the time of shift changes and, because I had time on my hands, I spent it familiarising myself with the workings of the mine.

You had to go down the mine because you needed to understand the language of the pit and so you could assess injuries. If a man strained his shoulder carrying a girder, or had a gullick chop land on his feet, it helped to know what exactly what he was talking about. I used to go down once a month with the safety officer just to know what was going on underground and what kind of conditions the men were working in. The first pit I went down was in the Frances Colliery. It was a bit like going into a factory but you could see the problems. I wasn't frightened but it was all right going down for two hours. I wouldn't like to be down there eight hours a day and five days a week. It's a bit claustrophobic and you can see how it might affect people, and also see the potential for injuries from roof falls, and pneumonoconiosis from the coal dust.

Since then, there's been a great transition in the nursing practice because I started off treating injuries then got interested in preventative medicine. Basically that's why I began going down with the safety officer, to see if there was anything we could do to prevent accidents. We looked at supplies of oxygen underground and of morphine - we had to train deputies how to use it. While I was there, we had a series of lime burns. Lime came from a kind of cement they used for roof supports, it got down inside the men's wellingtons and gave nasty burns. We looked at the problem and came up with a code of practice which the mines inspectors took up, and eventually the code was made policy throughout the Coal Board. I was delighted that I was playing a preventative role and not just sticking plasters on.

To begin with I got bad vibes from the management because I was creating precedents, but I had the respect of the men. There were no problems with men objecting to women, in fact the opposite was true. They weren't used to having a full time nurse and when I went there first, they were coming in with sore heads, sore throats, anything – just as an excuse to have a look at the new nurse. Nurses were always respected, them men knew their lives might depend on us in an emergency.

A funny thing happened my first week at Solsgirth. A miner was injured and the report that came up the pit was that he was unconscious with head injuries. We had an ambulance standing by when they brought him up. We loaded him in and I went with him to the East Fife Hospital in Dunfermline. Fortunately he wasn't badly hurt, just dazed. A few days later, I had a report of an engineer with a broken ankle. I could see the men were not very happy with my treatment but nobody said anything. On the Monday morning, however, I had a visit from the union representative, wanting to know why I was discriminating against the engineer because I didn't have an ambulance waiting for him though I had one for the miner.

I explained that a broken ankle is not life-threatening and it was better that we got his wet clothes off, cut off his wellington boots and sent him to the hospital comfortable in clean dry clothes. After that I decided to 'think union'. If I did anything different, I'd go to the union first, explain what I was doing and why I was doing it.

We had to work with the Mines Rescue people and if there was an accident we would be sent to the mine involved, so twenty – four hour medical cover could be provided if necessary. In my four years, there were three deaths, two heart attacks and one accident. It was the helplessness of the situation that was stressful. I was on the surface and the sick or injured man was underground and it might take stretcher bearers one or two hours to get him out. One always wondered if they would have survived if they had been nearer medical help. The first aiders did their best of course, with instructions by telephone from the medical centre. When the patient was brought out we had to go through the motions of resuscitation, knowing full well it was too late. A local doctor would be called to certify death and the police also had to be informed. It was a very traumatic experience for all concerned and in respect for the dead man, his shift mates would stay off work the following day.

As well as treating injuries we treated coughs and colds and minor illnesses and a vaccination programme was introduced for tetanus. The nurse was also a confidant, where employees could off-load their troubles, be they social, marital, financial or whatever. We would hear about the hatches, matches and dispatches, give general advice on health matters and discuss lifestyle issues such as alcohol, smoking and diet. We gave stamina and fitness tests and assisted the doctors giving medicals to new employees . By the 1970s, occupational health had come into its own with the idea of a treatment service moving towards prevention rather than cure, so we began to do lung function teats and hearing tests. It was difficult to do health education because of the underground work but we had posters and leaflets about smoking, drinking and so on. The nurses also assisted in the training of medical room attendants by hands-on example in the medical centre, and also their formal training in a residential setting. We also had our own in-service days in the form of a meeting with the two medical officers.

There were surface workers to deal with as well, joiners, storemen and the management team, a secretary, women in the canteen, and the girls who were in involved in paying out wages each week. I trained the first aiders because I felt their training had not been sufficient and we went in for competitive training, competing against teams from other collieries, the police and fire service. I needed that for motivation purposes, it would have been very easy to sit around waiting for an accident to happen. I'd go along on a Saturday to watch the teams compete, and went to Blackpool to support them when they reached the national finals for the whole of the coal industry. I used to man the first aid tent with them on gala days.

I really enjoyed my work but I wanted to learn more about industrial diseases like pneumonoconiosis, the effects of dust and chemicals, skin problems and so on. I applied to go on a course in Occupational Health but the management would not allow me to go, though later nurses were able to do the course on day release. So I left and gained the qualification for Occupational Health in Industry, then went to Bangour Hospital and set up the Occupational Health Service for West Lothian. Because few people had the qualifications, I rattled up the promotion ladder to become Manager of the Service for Glasgow. I retired when the hospital trusts took over and now run my own consultancy business.

LINDA CRAIG

By the time Linda Craig began working in industry in 1979, coal mining in Scotland was still very much a viable concern. Having worked in various industries including Mossmorran and the Civil Service, she returned to the NHS as an Occupational Health nurse at a time when it was undergoing vast changes in structure, and senior nurses were being retired early in droves. As one of those who was forced to take early retirement at fifty she wasn't ready to give up working. She joined an agency which eventually led to her being employed as Nursing Officer at Longannet Colliery in Mining , another industry which had almost been obliterated. When she took over in 1994 she inherited three staff nurses and a medical centre that operated twenty four hours a day. When Castlebridge Access was run down in early 2000 the whole team moved to Longannet Access.

'When British Coal decided to stop providing medical services, the staff set up an independent company, Business Health Care, which is based in Mansfield in Nottingham and I am employed by them on contract to Scottish Coal, Deep Mine, the only deep mine left in Scotland and Opencast. As well as the Longannet complex, I'm responsible for medical care on open cast sites belonging to Scottish Coal but have nothing to do with other privately owned sites.

The work force is about six hundred but numbers fluctuate and I deal with everything to do with health and safety. A lot of my work involves health screening - routine medical checks for drivers, skin checks for anyone working with chemicals underground, audiometry and lung function tests. The doctor, who is also female, holds a clinic every week doing pre-employment medicals, which new people coming in have to undergo if they are not already on the contractor's list. She also sees people who have been off sick for a long time. Throughout the coal industry, anyone who has a contract with Business Health Care is offered four-yearly routine X-rays to keep checks on their dust levels.

We didn't think we had a problem here with pneumonoconiosis but it appears we have, though protective masks are compulsory and the dust levels are well controlled. Many of the men have come from other collieries and have missed their routine checks, some have gone eight to twelve years without an X-ray. Problems can be picked up early and then we recommend that they work only in specified dust levels and do no overtime. As the disease progresses, they have to work in virtually dust free conditions. There is no cure, there are no early symptoms and if men left the industry the disease would not progress so in fact they are taking a calculated risk ;but sickness and death is not as much part of the job as it used to be.

By its nature, the job is not as safe and workers don't have such healthy conditions as in a factory, for example, but we make it as safe as we possibly can. We go underground only to visit unless we are looking for something specific, to see how a job is done and can highlight problems to the Health and Safety Executive. They also alert us to possible problems. We go down occasionally for accidents, mostly minor because safety is so paramount that the kind of injuries I used to see in the Accident and Emergency Unit in the old West Fife Hospital just don't happen any more. Injuries to hand and fingers are common and back strain, of course, but even since 1993, the accident rate has decreased and luckily there's been only one fatality during my time here. Coal seams are high and the roadways are as big as houses. It just so happened that the last time we had an accident and the injured man had to be stretchered out, the men from Scotland's only Mines Rescue Station at Crossgates were there so it was a good training exercise for them. Most miners have some First Aid training carried out by Mines rescue which I have to examine, because there is a difference between First Aid in Mines and First Aid at Work. Miners traditionally have been superb, and teams from mines nationally competed with each other. Today our team competes with other industries - Scottish Gas, Scottish Power and the Police for example - and have kept the cup. Our male nurse works with the Red Cross and St John's Ambulance so he's in the team as well.

We had a visit recently from the chest physician and respiratory nurses from the Victoria Hospital who wanted to see for themselves the working conditions of their patients. The men love having visitors and are very protective towards people who go down. Medical staff have to make an underground visit when they begin but as a rule we are too busy with the treatment centre. Longannet is the only mine where they have four nurses providing a round the clock service. Most pits in the south have one nurse covering several collieries with the help of medical attendants and medical centres are not open twenty four hours a day. These attendants are highly trained but the management here insisted on having trained nurses, who work shifts Monday to Friday and are on call over the weekend. Two of the nurses formed their own company which is under contract to the colliery and they employ the third member of staff, who is male. When they started to bring in staff nurses, my predecessor always had one man on the staff because medical attendants had always been male, and I thought it was good to keep it that way.

I work eight till four, do routine jobs and lots of administration. Nurses roles have changed over the years. To begin with, they were called industrial nurses and not expected to do very much. The service was very much accident orientated, now we are more into health surveillance. We are one of the few industries that provide a big treatment service but in general we don't see our work force, except during shift changes or when there's problems. At other times they are working out of sight below ground but they know there is always someone here to listen to problems.'

When Linda Craig began working with Scottish Coal in 1994, there were still mines at Castlebridge, Castlehill and Solsgirth, operating as part of the Longannet Complex. Seven years later only Longannet remains, with the Castlebridge site earmarked as the headquarters building for the industry. Coal is brought in from open cast sites to be mixed with that from deep mining and cheap coal is being imported. Longannet was expected to have a continued commercial existence for at least another twenty years, but in the 1950s, Fife Council had confidently envisaged a mining work force of over twenty thousand by the end of the century.

By December 2000, Longannet was in deep trouble. It suffered serious losses because of a series of geological faults and from being in competition with subsidised pits in Germany, France and Spain. The colliery was saved from closure by a subsidy of seventeen and a half million pounds from the European Commission. It was hailed as the best possible present for the six hundred and fifty workers, but further grants will probably be necessary if Longannet is to continue as a viable proposition.

Meantime, Linda Craig holds a unique position as the only nursing officer in the coal industry in Scotland. There are other female Scottish Coal employees, of course, receptionists, secretaries, canteen and switchboard assistants, but Linda, her two nurses and the Medical Officer are the only women whose work involves direct contact with underground working.

Miners and pit head workers at Bowhill Colliery

EPILOGUE

Scotland was not the only country where women were employed as slave labour. Though they didn't work underground, women in Wales wore leather straps round their wrists and these were attached to coal trams which were used at opencast workings on hillsides. 1911, the year which saw the last attempt to ban pit head working in Britain also saw the banning of females underground in Belgium. Until 1883 when the practice was banned, women had worked in harness and at that time around seven thousand females were employed in Belgian deep mines.

In 1935 The International Labour Organisation proposed a ban in Europe, Canada and Australia but in the 1970s, Chinese and Japanese and Indian women were still employed underground. Japan had a female work force of over forty four thousand in 1930. In America women only began mining this century but numbers were minimal till the passing of anti discrimination legislation in 1974. By the end of the decade over two and a half thousand women were working underground, some leading mining teams and others becoming presidents of their local unions.

In this country, the 1989 Equal Opportunities legislation made it possible for women to work underground again, but by that time, the opportunities for any miner, male or female, were few and far between. In the pit villages, women still mourn the demise of the coal industry. Comfortable, clean living conditions, a return to an agricultural, rural countryside and the removal or landscaping of unsightly coal bings are weighed against a way of life that had been handed down for generations, and found wanting. No-one could mourn the freedom from danger, from the sense of always living on the edge of a precipice; but when the pits went, the heart of the community went, too.

In the last years of the twentieth century, new industries such as electronics were suitable for women workers but no procedures were put in place to find work for men. Defeat by the government in 1984 meant exactly that. Families, whose lives had revolved around the pits since time out of mind, saw their livelihood and way of life wiped out almost overnight. Social structures changed, people's place in their society was no longer clear cut. Some of the pit villages have vanished, others are now dormitory towns or have changed out of recognition. The local authority housing which replaced the miners rows is now being replaced by housing estates and newcomers, though welcomed, still remain to some extent outsiders.

The women, as always, adapt to changing circumstance, living in the present rather than harking back to a less than ideal past, thankful for washing machines, central heating and a regular, if sometimes meagre income. Soon the past will be another country, attainable only through books and museums; but some things should be remembered. Apart from the land itself, coal was the only national resource the country had. Britain's wealth, her place as the foremost industrial nation in the world, the development of steam driven machinery, trains and ships could not have happened without the work of the miners, male and female.

For over four hundred years, however, mining families, central to the economic well being of the country, were regarded as a threat to its stability. The whole history of mining is a long war between people demanding the right to work in reasonably safe conditions for a reasonable living wage, and the coal owners whose concern for profitability outweighed considerations of safety and humanity. The protagonists were unevenly matched. Miners had only their labour and their pride, their opponents could call on the full might of the law, the government and the military.

The legacy of the pit remains, the old men with emphysema and blue scarred skin; the Goths, the bowling greens and miners institutes - though most of these are now run by local authorities as Community Centres. Here and there is a mining wheel or a coal hutch, set up as a memorial to the industry that died.

There are memorials, too, to the men who were killed, but no monuments to the women who died. Even though the numbers are small in comparison, they do exist and ought to be acknowledged. Too often, women's role has been overlooked. History, they say is written by the victors. One woman, Margaret Thatcher, confident of her own place in history, claimed in 1984 that she had won, though the value of a victory that destroys the industrial fabric and the social heart of a country is doubtful. For mining women, it is time to reclaim, not victory certainly, but at least some credit for being part of the battle.

The end of a long story.
Women receive plaques to commemorate their involvement in support groups in Fife.

NOTES

Introduction

1. Children's Employment Commission. (CEC) Its full title was *'An Inquiry into the Employment of Children of the Poorer Classes in Mines and Collieries, and the various branches of trade and manufacture in which numbers of Children work together, not being included in the provisions of the Acts for regulating the Mills and Factory.'*
2. Tom Johnston *Our Scots Noble Families - A General Indictment p vii*

Chapter One

1. Acts of The Scottish Parliament 1364
2. P. MacNeill - *Tranent and its Surroundings*
3. Rothes Papers - quoted in Kirkcaldy Technical College *A Preliminary Investigation into the Industrial Archaeology of Fife*
4. George Montgomery, *A Mining Chronicle*
5. Lord Henry Cockburn *Memorials of His Time*
6. Tom Johnston *A History of the Working Classes in Scotland* p84
7. Ivy Pinchbeck *Women Workers and the Industrial Revolution* p240
8. R. L. Galloway *Annals of Coal Mining and the Coal Trade* p11
9. Lord Cockburn *Memorials of His Time*
10. Acts of The Scottish Parliament 1641
11. Children's Employment Commission
12. Peter W. Brown - *History of Coal Mining in Lochgelly*
13. Balfour of Balbirnie Muniments quoted in S.R.O *The Coalminers*
14. Henderson of Fordell Muniments quoted in S.R.O *The Coalminers*
15. Rothes Papers, quoted in Kirkcaldy Technical College *Industrial Archaeology*
16. *ibid*
17. George Montgomery *A Mining Chronicle*
18. Quoted in Hugh Miller *My Schools and Schoolmasters* . I am grateful to James Robertson for introducing me to Hugh Miller's work
19. Thomas Johnston *History of The Working Classes in Scotland p348*

Chapter Two:

1. Hamilton of Pencaitland Papers quoted in S.R.O. *The Coalminers*
2. Archibald Cochrane *A Description of the Abbey and Estate of Culross*
3. Glasgow Herald 15/8/1859
Most of the information in this chapter comes from CEC

Chapter Three:

1. B.R.S Megaw *Women Coal Bearers in a Midlothian Mine* Scottish Studies Vol.10
2. Matthias Dunn *The Edge Coals of Midlothian*
3. Robert Gillespie *Round About Falkirk* p248
5. Archibald Cook *A Human Document* in *The Jenny Gray Centenary Book*
Other quotes from CEC

Chapter Four:

1. *Considerations of the Present Scarcity and High prices of Coal*
2. J. L. Carvel *One Hundred Years in Coal*
3. Friedrich Engels *The Condition of the Working Classes in England* p 255
4. Quoted in A.V. John *By The Sweat of Their Brow* p48

Chapter Five

1. CEC
2. Collieries Act 1842
3. A. V. John *By The Sweat of Their Brow* p37
4. *ibid* p51
5. *ibid* p.53
6. Quoted in Anthony Burton *The Miners*
7. George Montgomery *A Mining Chronicle*
8. Michael Hiley *Victorian Working Women, Portraits From Life* p89
9. A.V. John *By The Sweat of Their Brow* p57
10. *ibid* p58

Chapter Six:

1. Friedrich Engels - *The Condition of the Working Classes in England* p 255
2. Parliamentary Papers 1842 XVI. p181 quoted A. V. John p 40
3 -12. CEC
13. Cochrane *A Description of the Abbey and Estate of Culross*
14. *ibid*
15. *ibid*
16. Hugh Miller - *My Schools and Schoolmasters*
17. *The Wishaw Press April 30 1874*
18. Anthony Burton *The Miners* p100
19. Alistair Findlay *Shale Voices*
20. Robert Brown *History of Coal Mining in Lochgelly*
21. George Montgomery *A Mining Chronicle*

22. CEC
23. *ibid*
24. Murdo Mackay and the Green Table
25. *ibid*
26. John Slatter (ed) *From The Other Shore p141*
27. *ibid p149*
28. Archibald Cochrane *A Description of the Abbey and Estate of Culross*
29. N.C.B Scottish Division *A Short History of The Coal Mining Industry*

Chapter Seven

1. A. V. John *By The Sweat of Their Brow* p53
2. Quoted in B. Job *British Mining* No 59
3. Michael Hiley *Victorian Working Women, Portraits From Life* p50
4 . John Plummer *Once A Week* XI 1864 quoted in A. V. John p133
5. Raphael. (ed) *Miners, Quarrymen and Salters*
6 Michael Hiley *Victorian Working Women, Portraits From Life*
7. ibid
8. Quoted in *A Mining Chronicle*
9. A. G. Campbell *Lanarkshire Miners*
10. A. V. John *By The Sweat of Their Brow* p180
11. *ibid* p183
12. *Ibid* p190
13. *ibid*
14. George Montgomery *A Mining Chronicle*
15. A. V. John *By The Sweat of Their Brow p168*
16. ibid *p172*
17. *Ibid p173*
18. *Interview with Margaret Rodger 1997*
19. F. H. Burnett *That Lass o Lowrie's*

Chapter Eight

1. J. Ronaldson *Mines Inspector's Report 1893*
2. *Commission of Employment of Women* 1892
3. Robert Holman *Character Studies of the Miners of West Fife* p7-8
4. Kellog Durland *My Life With the Miners* p57-58
5. *ibid* p58
6. *ibid* p98
7. *ibid* p116
8. *ibid* p105

9. ibid p108

10. T. C. Smout *A History of the Scottish People* p103

11. Wm. D. Henderson *Townhill, Dunfermline's Coal Town*

12. Carnegie Trust Dunfermline *Scottish Mothers and Children*

13. Report of The Royal Commission on Housing

14. ibid

15. ibid

16. ibid

17. Scottish Shale Miners Association *Housing Conditions in the Scottish Shale Field*

18. Report of Scottish Home Department on Scottish Coalfields 1944

19. Abe Moffatt - *My Life With The Miners* p10

20. ibid p11

Chapter Nine

1. The Glasgow Journal quoted in James D. *Young Women and Popular Struggles*

2. ibid

3. Wanlockhead Museum Trust   *All About Wanlockhead*

4. Ian Fenton *Chartism in Clackmannanshire* Scottish Local History Journal No 37

5. *ibid*

6. A.G Campbell *Lanarkshire Miners* p162

7. *Ibid* p162

8. Brian Murphy *ASLEF 1880 - 1980*

9. A.V. John *By The Sweat of Their Brow* p149

10. *ibid* p153

11. Quoted in Leah Leneman *A Guid Cause* p61

12. Letter to The Times 1912

13. West Lothian Courier April 1916

14. Alastair Findlay *Shale Voices*

15. Stirling Women's Oral Project

16. *ibid*

17. I am grateful to W.S. Harvey, retired curator of Wanlockhead Museum for this information

Chapter Ten

1. Iain Johnston   *Women in the Communist Party in Fife Between The Wars*

2. *ibid*

3. Bob Selkirk *The Life of a Worker* p17

4. Community Heritage Project *Cowie, A Mining Village*

5. Bob Selkirk *The Life of a Worker*   p29

6. *ibid* p27

7. *ibid*

8. Iain Johnston *Women in the Communist Party Between the Wars*

9. Mary Docherty interview 1997

10. Mary Docherty . Interview   1999

11. Dunfermline Press

12. N.U.M *A Century Of Struggle*

13. Alastair Findlay *Shale Voices*

14. Abe Moffatt *My Life With The Miners* p59 –60

15. Jennie Lee *My Life With Nye*

16. Anni Cairns. I am indebted to Audrey Canning of the STUC Library for letting me have access to this testimony

17. Helen Crawfurd's unpublished autobiography. I am also indebted to Audrey Canning for access to this material.

Chapter 11.

All quotes in this chapter are from the Stirling Women's Oral Project

Chapter 12.

1. Grit and Diamonds p42

2. *ibid* p43

3. Living The Strike p10

4. Never the Same Again

5. Living The Strike

6. *ibid*

7. A Very Hard Year p 18

8. Living The Strike p34

9.A Very Hard Year p9

10 ibid

11. Grit and Diamonds p43

12. A Very Hard Year p24

Chapter 13

Transcripts of taped interviews

Barbara Marshall interviewed September 2000, all other pit head workers 1997

Chapter 14

Taped interviews

Elsie Brodie – February 2000

Linda Craig – September 2000

BIBLIOGRAPHY

The Children's Employment Commission 1840
The Collieries Act 1842
The Coal Mines Regulation Act 1872
Amendment to Coal Mines Regulation Act 1886
Select List of British Parliamentary Papers   Percy Ford 1953

T. C. Smout *A History of The Scottish People* 1560 –1730 Fontana 1972
Thomas Johnston A *History of The Working Classes in Scotland* Forward Publishing 1920
Thomas Johnston *Our Noble Scots Families*   Forward publishing 1926
Robert Bald *A General View of The Coal Trade of Scotland* Edinburgh 1808
Archibald Cochrane *A Description of the Abbey And Estate of Culross*   1793
Matthias Dunn *Notice of the Edge Seams of Midlothian*
Lord Henry Cockburn *Memorials of His Time*   1856
P. MacNeill *Tranent and its Surroundings*   1883
Hugh Miller *My Schools and Schoolmasters*   1854
Friedrich Engels *The Condition of the Working Class in England* 1844.
Alex Westwater *Alex Westwater's Lochgelly* Alex Westwater Memorial Trust 1994
Wm. D. Henderson *Townhill, Dunfermline's Coaltown* Carnegie Dunfermline Trust 1981
George Montgomery *A Mining Chronicle* Newcraighall Heritage Society 1994
Vic Allen *The Militancy of British Miners*   Shipley 1981
John Benson *British Coalmen in the 19th Century*   Dublin 1980
Ian McDougall *Militant Miners* Polygon Books 1981
A. G. Campbell *The Lanarkshire Miners*
R .L. Galloway *Annals of Coalmining and the Coal Trade*   Newton Abbot 1971
N.C.B. Scottish Division *A Short History of the Coal Mining Industry* 1958
Ed. Raphael *Miners, Quarrymen and Saltworkers*   Routledge Kegan Paul 1977
T. Stewart *Among The Miners*   Larkhall 1893
Stuart Macintyre *Little Moscows*   1980
Abe Moffatt *My Life With The Miners*   London 1965
R. A. Houston *Coal, Class and Culture*
Anthony Burton *The Miners*   Andre Deutsch   1976
Scottish Record Office *The Coalminers*   1983
National Union of Mineworkers *A Century of Struggle*   1989
Leslie C Wright *Scottish Chartism*   Oliver & Boyd 1953
John L. Carvel *One Hundred Years in Coal, The History of the Alloa Coal Company* Constable 1944
John L Carvel *The New Cumnock Coal Field, A Record of its Development and Activities* Constable 1946

Cowie, A Mining Village   Community Heritage Programme 1986

Billy Kay (ed) *Odyssey Volume One* Polygon Books 1980

Bob Selkirk *The Life of a Worker* - (now reprinted in *Auld Bob Selkirk, A Man in a Million*, Mary Docherty 1996)

Alistair Findlay *Shale Voices*   Luath Press 1999

Derek Hudson *Munby, Man of Two Worlds*   John Murray 1972

A. V John *Coalmining Women, Victorian Lives and Campaigns* C.U.P. 1984

A. V. John *By The Sweat Of Their Brow*   Routledge, Keegan, Paul 1984

Ivy Pinchbeck *Women Workers in the Industrial Revolution*   George Routledge & Sons 1930

Michael Hiley *Working Victorian Women, Portraits From Life* Gordon Fraser 1979

W.F. Neff *Victorian Working Women*   Allen & Unwin 1929

Duncan Crow *The Victorian Woman*   Allen & Unwin 1971

James D. Young *Women and Popular Struggles*   Edinburgh 1985

Barbara Drake *Women in Trades Unions*   Virago 1984

L. Tilly and J. Scott *Women, Work and Family* London 1987

Leah Leneman *A Guid Cause*   Mercat Press 1995

S. Henderson and A. Mackay *Grit and Diamonds Women in Scotland Making History 1980 – 90*

Lothian Women's Support Group *Women Living The Strike*   1986

J. Stead *Never The Same Again*   Woman's Press 1987

John Slatter (ed) *From The Other Shore, Russian Emigrants in Britain*

J. Millar *The Lithuanians In Scotland*   1988

Ian MacDougall *Murdo McKay and the Green Table* Tuckwell Press 1995

Alex Maxwell *Chicago Tumbles*   *1994*

Miscellaneous:

Helen Crawfurd *Unpublished Autobiography*

Carnegie Dunfermline U.K. Trust on Physical Welfare 1917 *Scottish Mothers and Children Volume Three*

B. Job *Women Workers in British Collieries and the Mines Inspectors* Northern Mine Research Society in British Mining Memoirs No. 59, 1977

Women's Social and Political Union pamphlets

Scottish Local History Volume 37 June 1996

Scottish Shale Miners Association 1914 *Housing Conditions In the Scottish Shale Field*

Report on the Sanitary Conditions of the Labouring Population of Scotland 1842

Inquiry into the Truck System Minutes of Evidence 1871

West Lothian Courier - various dates

Dunfermline Press - various dates

The Wishaw Press – 30/5/74

The Glasgow Herald – various dates

PICTURE ACKNOWLEDGEMENTS

Pictures are reproduced by kind permission of the following:

Dunfermline Press – p69,79,
Children's Employment Commission sketches – pp
6,8,12,14,16,17,18,20,21,24,27,29
Fife Council Libraries Collections – p4 lower, 34,48,49,51,57, 60,72, 83 upper, 88,
90, 101, 103, 106 lower, 107,124
Smith Institute and Museum Collection – p4 upper
West Lothian Local Libraries Collection - p 37, 39, 54, 66,71, 78, 109
(54 copyright Mrs J Tennant ; 66, 109 copyright the late John Kelly)
North Lanarkshire Council, Museums and Heritage Collection – 43, 116
Falkirk Libraries Collection - 39,46, back cover
Scottish Trades Union Congress Library –p64, 75, 83 lower
Ann Eden – p 106, lower
Janice Russell – 96,100,126
Mary Docherty – 76

Efforts have been made to contact all copyright holders. Where acknowledgement is
missing, the publishers will be pleased to rectify this in later editions.

ABOUT THE WRITER

Lillian King is a graduate of Edinburgh University. Most of her career has been in
Adult Education and she is now a part time tutor with the WEA in Fife, teaching
local history and creative writing. Her particular interests are railways, mining and
women's history. She edits and produces *Fife Fringe*, an arts and literary magazine
and has edited several anthologies of poetry.
Previous books include:

A Railway Childhood
The Last Station
Thornton Railway Days
Famous Women of Fife